CAROLINA:

OR,

Loyal Poems.

By *Tho. Shipman*, Esq;.

LONDON,

Printed for *Samuel Heyrick*, at *Grayes-Inn-Gate* in *Holborn*, and *William Crook*, at the *Green Dragon* without *Temple-Bar*. 1683.

ISBN 0 576 02247 0

Republished in 1971 by Gregg International Publishers Limited
Westmead, Farnborough, Hants., England

Printed in offset by Franz Wolf,Heppenheim/Bergstrasse
Western Germany

THE
PREFACE.

THis *Preface* wants the accuftom'd
pretence for thefe *Trifles* appear-
ing in Print. No *Friends* advis'd
to it. It was merely in obedience to
that *Genius*, which both beftow'd and
over-fway'd my Youthful *Fancy*. So
that mine Excufe may th' eafilier be
admitted, fince Duty and Conftraint
joyn'd Forces againft me. I muft
confefs, I lov'd *Poetry* not only then,
but do fo ftill; and am fo loving a Soul,
that I hate not even my *Rivals*. Let
em woo and enjoy, I muft love on.

The Preface.

I know not, indeed, whether I should
be so good natur'd, to continue constant after a *dry beating* or two, though
even that cannot prevail with some
of us. Not so much to have made
Verses, as not to give over in time,
leaves us without excuse, sayes an
excellent *Poet*. I dissent from *M.W.*
his observation. Methinks it looks like
the gelding of Fancy; and he might
as well have set a time after which it
should be criminal to lye with our
Wives. Another, * as eminent, * *M. D.*
calls them *Fumblers* who write after
forty. But I hope he will fumble on
still, having put us in expectation of
an *Epick Poem*, which (like *Solomon*)
must be the *Darling* of his Age, and
out-wit his other *Brethren*. I see no
cause but *Dotage* to make it be left off.
Socra-

The Preface.

Socrates and *Solon* practis'd it to the laft; and one as wife as either of 'em left it for a Rule, *Quomodo proficis, fi jam tibi sufficis? S. Bern.* The progreffions of Fancy are to be waited on. Experience and repetitions of multiply'd *Acts* being as neceffary here as in other *Sciences. Seneca* tells us, *Nihil eft magnum re quod breve tempore.*

Yet fome other Confiderations prevail'd; For, firft, they were not made upon mine own account; I having no more concern than Mafter-Builders, whofe pleafure lafts only in the *Working.* Nor fhall the Reader or I hereby receive greater benefit than the freeing me from *Tranfcribing,* and him from *Reading* a bad *Hand.* Nor am I farther follicitous for them, fince moft of thofe for whom thefe were written are

al-

already satisfied. For, methinks, I ought not disparage their Judgments, there being rationally (or at least civilly) to be expected, from mine *Acquaintance*, as good *Judges* as elsewhere. And I cannot but know, that as many things have been printed of this nature much better, so some a little worse.

The name of *Poet* I neither slight nor covet. And may be one of the main motives to appear so, is, that I cannot avoid it ; being already in Print recorded so by a * Learned * *D.T.* hand ; though I am to expect as little credit thereby, as happily that *Author* has gain'd by his Work : Nor indeed could much be expected, where room was for such Trifles. Another motive was, my natural propensity to *Love* and *Friendship* ; which in their

se-

The Preface.

several circumstances make up those curious lines that compose the beauty of *Honour*; whose charms are so far powerful, they have attracted regards from the *Heroes* of all Ages. Herein I have such a tenderness, I would gladly leave something of me surviving to record it. But this I would provide for in my Life-time, being little satisfied with *posthumous Dedications*; which serve but as *Monuments* rais'd by *Executors*, where their Names are sure to shine in the fairest Characters. That slender Estate of *Repute* I am able to compass, being too small for any to come in as *Joynt-Purchaser*: and I may be as far out in this bargaining as Captain *Frobisher*, who, after a long and chargeable Voyage, brought home *worthless Stones*, for *precious Minerals*;

A 4   and

and what he hop'd might have been graced as *Jewels* for the Ears of *Ladies*, were us'd as *Pavements* for the Streets.

Nor may my lanching out into the wide World, and incountering the *Tide* of *Criticks*, bring any folider Account than *Caligula's* Attempt upon the Ocean, when his *Trophies* were only a few *Cockle-shells*. Neither can I make a furer ghefs, whether in pruning or lopping many fuperfluous Branches, thofe that are left may bring me better Fruit. This may be believed; If my *Soil* had been improv'd equal to fome others, it might have produced better things. But inftead of that Incouragement, not only the *Favour* of the *Sun*, but the very *Dew* of the *Night* were deny'd me.

Pectora

The Preface.

Pectora nostra duas non admittentia curas;
Magnæ mentis opus, nec de Lodice paranda
Attonitæ, Currus & Equos, faciesque Deorum
Aspicere. ———

Such advantages might have better'd *Nature.* For though it agrees with the boasted Nobleness of a *Poet*'s Soul to rest satisfied with his own Fame justly acquired; yet,

Contentus fama jaceat Lucanus in hortis
Marmoreis. ----

Pleasant *Retirements* produce pleasant Thoughts, and noble Injoyments heighten the Sentiments of any *Writer.* A fuller Stream than *Helicon*'s may be drain'd that has no *Showers* to supply the *Current*; nor will it be worth the while, if we believe a sort of People, who injoy so small a share of Wit to think

think they have enough. Some of thefe tells us, that the *Mufes*, like *Syrens*, infatuate their Admirers, and charm them into Ruine; that *Poetry* foftens our Minds, making them unable for more mafculine Operations. Yet fome of them fhew fo much Inclination to the *Mufes*, that they whiftle out their Souls at the *Plow-tail*, having little more title to Reafon than *Brutes*; who can judge only of a fat Pafture, chew the Cud, and batten. Their generous Educations may have rais'd 'em to read badly, and write worfe. Hence are they capacitated to blot a *Bond*, and manage an *Arbitration*, untill they fwell and arrogate to themfelves an Ability for *Empire*. If it were not loft labour to preach to fuch an *Audience*, they might

might be inftructed, how in all Ages *Philofophers, Priefts, Law-makers,* and *Kings,* have facrific'd to the *Mufes:* And in their time th' incomparable *Verulam* and juft *Hales,* (to name no more) heighten'd their Thoughts by this way of writing. Here I could expatiate, but I purpofely avoid it, it being in fome fort a Difparagement to praife a celebrated *Perfection* too publickly. Nor fhall I run into that arrogating Cuftom of judging others, and impofing Rules that neither we nor others endeavour to practife. *Fancy* fhould be unconfin'd as the *Air,* and the *Mufes,* like *Amazons,* fcorn the Rule even of a *Cyrus. Helicon* (like their *Thermodon*) being the *Boundary* of their *Empire,* not permitting any other Streams to imbody with

its

its chryftal Waves; but, like *Jordan*, forces its fhining Current quite through the *Dull Sea* of *Pedantifm*, over-bearing all that reftrains the Liberty of its natural Progrefs.

Yet after all this, we muft confefs, that *Poets* would gladly be entertain'd in more profitable Imployments; fo to affert the bounty of *Nature* in beftowing upon them as vigorous Capacities as other People; and convincing the World they were capable of Affairs of moment, would it be fo courteous to make Tryal (may be) to both their Advantages.

TO

TO THE

READER.

Kind Reader,

THE *Ingenious Author of the following Compositions was a Man every way accomplish'd: To the advantages of his Birth, his Education had added whatsoever was necessary to fit him for Conversation, and render him (as he was) desirable by the best Wits of the Age. In the Calamities of the last Rebellion he was no small Sharer, the Iniquity of the Times having no*

power

power to *shock* his *Loyalty,* he very
cheerfully underwent the *Tryals* of un-
happy *Virtue.* In that *miserable* Storm
it was his good *Fortune* to retire from a
total *Ruine* ; and that quiet *Recess* gave
the opportunity of these *Papers,* in which
thou wilt find many *troublesome* thoughts
well *digested,* and perhaps, at *some* time
or other, well enough adapted to thy
own *uneasie Circumstances.* If there be
any thing *meaner* than may be expected
from so polite a *Pen,* thy *Candor* must
attribute it either to the *hasty Efforts* of
his younger, or the *too* ponderous and
over-pow'ring *Confusions* which the *Rebellion* imprinted on his riper *Years.* He
is dead, and happy out of the reach of
thy *Envy,* and in no need of thy *Pity;*
therefore (*Good Reader*) for *Humanity*
sake be charitable to the *Productions* of

a dead

To the Reader.

a dead Author, who was worthily ho-
nour'd and admir'd while he lived, and
attain'd the defirable Satisfaction of li-
ving very eafily in a troublefome Age,
and carrying with him a good Confcience
to his Grave.

Feb.7.
$168\frac{2}{3}$

Tho. Flatman.

A Modeft

A Modeſt Account of the too-certain Reaſons that afforded time for the following Trifles. 1779.

SOME *Females* are ſo early pregnant grown,
  They rock thoſe *Cradles* lately were their own.
  Their *Nurſe's milk* wants time, and ſcarce digeſts;
  And what they ſuckt, *unturn'd* comes from their
But ſoon, like *Spaniſh Wifes*, they barren grow; (*Breaſts.*
Their *Springs* are drain'd when ours begin to flow.
And happy 'tis --- elſe we ſhould be undone,
And by our *Native Vandals* over-run.
Although my *Muſe* begun to bear betimes,
Still at this *Age* her *Courſes* keeps in *Rhymes.*
What *Pliny* writes of *Mares* of *Spaniſh* kind,
She's pregnant with no *Stallion*, but the *Wind.*
When e're that *airy Pegaſus* but blew,   * Of whom
My *Muſe* more fruitful than * *Phillira* grew   ('tis feign'd)
Fruitful as *Flies* in Summer; tho the gain   the *Centaur*
Prove ſmall, to boaſt theſe *maggots* of the *Brain.*   was gotten.
Should all this *Spawn* of *Helicon* but live,
The *Frogs* in *Egypt* did leſs trouble give.
This *Brood*, like *Conies*, hardly are deſtroy'd ;
The *Warren* proſpers on *Parnaſſus* ſide.
In whoſe increaſe ſmall benefit is found ;
And little elſe thrives in the haunted ground.

ſ: ℛ. B. 9   'Tis

'Tis labour loft to till a barren *Soil*;
When no *Returns*, but *Weeds*, requite the toil.
Yet weeded well before the *Seedlings* fhed,
They make the *Land* more *mellow*, where they bred;
And Vouchers are that other things than *Weeds*
Would profper there, if fown with better *Seeds.*
Nature will work: and would not own a lofs;
The fteril'ft *Soils* unfown will bring forth *Mofs.*
If not improv'd, fhe's ruin'd; Truths confefs
That *Canaan* now is turn'd a *Wildernefs.*

The ROYALIST.

Upon Crefwick *Dean of* St. J. C. C---*ordering Verfes for the Victory at* Worcefter. 1651.

IS't not enough to make our *Purfes* pay,
 Affefsments on our whole *Eftates* to lay?
But *Taxes* muft on our *Opinions* 'rife,
Nay, and our *Wits* be forc'd to pay *Excife?*
Harfh Laws! fince *Sack* pays *Cuftom* when't comes in,
Diftill'd in *Verfe*, muft it be taxt agin?
But now a *Victory* is got; what then?
Muft we write *Ballads* at the death of men,
Like *London*-Wits? who deck each *Tyburn*-Herfe,
And execute men o're again in Verfe?
Are we *Death's Chaplains*, that we muft be preft
To give thanks after fuch a bloody Feaft?
In *Baal's new Priefts* that Office only lies,
Where Blood is mingled with their *Sacrifice.*

The

The Royal MARTYR.

Upon the Martyrdom of that Glorious Prince Charles *the* Firft, *King of* Great Britain, &c. *Who died* Jan. 30. 1648. *Written* Jan. 30. 1652.

GReat *Solomon*, not circumfcrib'd to Rules,
  Freed from the flavifh Method of the Schools;
No more than Air (that Libertine) confin'd,
And no lefs comprehenfive was his mind;
The fhining fruit of *Eden* was his meat,
Which without curfe, or furfeit he did eat.
In Proverbs he his wifdom often fhrouds :
As *Phœbus* fometimes wears a Cloak of Clouds.
Their knowledg wifeft Nations thus convey'd,
And in fuch Cabinets their Jewels laid.
And thefe are fome of Ours --, *viz.* Night follows **Day**
And pureft Gold is leffen'd by Allay.

Both of the Morals are but one great truth,
Be'ng fully prov'd i'th' fortune of my Youth :
For when great *Charls* fell, by untimely fate,
The glorious *Martyr* both of *Church* and *State*;
His Sacred Blood, by bafeft *Rebels* fpilt,
Befprinkled all the *Nation* o'er with guilt.
Some with that fcarlet Sin are fpread all o're :
As Plagues are known by the inflaming Sore.
Nor ftaies it there---like to the leprous Jew,
The infection creeps into their Houfes too.
'Twill moulter them to duft ! the fpreading *Stains*
Flow (with the Seed) into their Children's *Veins*.

        By

By fome notorious Brand upon them fhow'n,
The guilt will be to future Ages known.
More than from Sin, none from the guilt is free'd ;
On ev'ry head the *Crimfon* fhow'r does bleed.
This *Scottifh Mift* wets all of us to th' skin ;
Some are fo rain'd on they are dous'd within.
A bleffed fhelter yet my Youth does bring:
Rains feldom fall, or gently in the Spring.
Yet from fome fhare of guilt, I can relieve
My felf no more, than from the crime of *Eve*,
But like *Orig'nal Sin*, It lefs appears ;
Long fince baptiz'd, and wafht away with tears.
My inn'cent youth, like to the fpringing Day,
Difperfes all defpairing fhades away.

The firft part of the *Proverb*'s fo far right.
But now, alas, I am o'rwhelm'd with night !
Thus in a harmlefs ftate of youth I ftood ;
I did no harm, but, ah! I did no good.
My influence, like to Winter Suns, did fhow ;
They fcortch not, but yet nothing make to grow.
To th' *Solftice* of my ftrength I may arrive,
And th' operations of my Soul will thrive.
If I to * *Brutus*'s glory may not come ;
I dare, with || *Curtius*, tempt a noble doom ;
And plunge into the Gulph to refcue *Rome*.
Cæfar's return we faithfully muft wait,
That time fhall come, I prophecy the fate
The *Prince* of *Judah* fhall return with praife,
Our *Temples* found, and facred *Altars* raife.
No more, till then, my mournful *Mufe* fhall fing,
Her *Harp* untun'd fhall on the *Willows* hing ;

* *Brutus* flew
the Tyrant ;
and || *Curtius*
to expiate
Romes guilt,
leapt into a
Gulph.

Un-

Unlefs it be to found fome doleful Airs;
To which I'l tune my Sighs, and teach my tears
A mournful cadence; until th' art be found,
To form fuch *Waterworks* into a *Sound.*
Ne'r jufter caufe! to fee the *Rabble* run,
Like *fteams* from *Dunghils* rais'd, to hide the *Sun.*
To fee rank *Poyfon* work in every part,
Until at laft its *Venom* feize the heart. || Witnefs E.
                                              Effex, Sir *Hen.*
To fee our royal *Oak,* (alas!) cut down,   *Mildmay, &c.*
And cleft with || *woodden wedges* of its own.
To fee great *Charls* before his *Palace* lye :
Like fate had once the *Sun,* when crown'd on high }
Arrefted in his very *Court,* the Sky.   }
But that was done by no ignoble hand;
It was at *Jofhua's* fuit the Sun did ftand.
But ours eclipft by hellifh *Vapours,* ftood,
And (as at th' end o' th' world) did *fet in Blood.*
Behold a mighty *Monarch* there lyes dead
Without his *Crown,* and (ah!) without his *Head!*
Expiring *Mufe!* with him receive thy doom,
And dye, like *Indian flaves,* upon his *Tomb.*
It is enough thou'ft thither him convey'd,
And in a *Tomb* of thine own framing laid.
All *Monuments* decay, and *Marbles* rot, ᛁ
Compar'd to th' *Quarries* in *Parnaffus* got.

 Thus the great *Pompey,* (who the World fubdu'd)
By *Rome's* ill fate, and *Tyrant's* force purfu'd,
Did to a *barb'rous Nation feek* for aid;
By them, to murd'ring *Villains,* was betray'd :
Headlefs expos'd on the *Pelufian* fhore
The *World's Head lay,* and all defil'd with gore!

By the dear Body faithful ||*Codrus* ſtood,   ¶His Slave.
And with his flowing tears waſht off the blood.
Then did interr the ſacred *Relicks* ſafe ;
Whoſe Piety is his beſt *Epitaph.*

Heroic *Lucan* has preſerv'd his fame,
Which bears an equal date with *Pompey*'s name ;
Well known to all that *World* he did ſubdue,
Flying as far, as *Pompey's Eagles* flew.

The GOWN.

Upon Sir Ward, *borrowing my Gown.* 1652.

I, Like *Philemon*, may *Jove's Fav'rite* be,
    In ſhelt'ring thus his darling-*Mercury.*
And yet I hated am, as once was *Lot,*
When *Angels* under his bleſt *Roof* he got.
Some think it thy diſparagement, to ſee
The Lord of Wit cloath'd in my Livery.
But here thy Worth unjuſtly they upbraid ;
Since *Kings* ſometimes are ſeen in *Maskarade.*
Nay 'tis well known, that heavenly *Forms* appear
In mortal ſhapes, or ſeem ſuch *Veils* to wear.
When next I put it on, for ought I know,
I may infected be, and witty grow.
Some influence muſt be left ; thus pretious *Gums*
Taken from *Boxes* leave their rich perfumes.
And I have read--He that did once inherit
Elija's, Mantle, got *Elija's Spirit.*

MODEST WORTH.

Upon the Death of Mr. R. Winterburn, *B. D.*
1652.

FOR flouds of tears this mournful fate does call;
  'Tis *Egypt* where (they fay) no fhowers fall.
Melt then your beams to tears, my thawing *Eyes*,
And *Heav'n* diffolves in *Dews*, when *Phœbus* dyes.
Alike they were ; for he long time did fway
The *Mufe's Scepter*, they did him obey.
Nay he excell'd in this-- for he was free
From any thought of *Daphne*, but her *Tree.*
Hi *Gold* lay clofe in 's *Mine* : His *Helicon*
Was full and deep; and fo did filent run.
This made fome flight him: *Stars* feem *Motes* i' th' *Skies* ;
Height leffens Objects to imperfect *Eyes.*
Yet none more lowly thought, or fpoke than he :
So rich mens cloaths perfuade a Poverty.
Plain *Scutcheons Heralds* look upon as beft ;
And *Maids* lofe credit that go lightly dreft ;
Di'monds in barren *Mountains* are infhrin'd ;
And *Popes* their *Sackcloth* wear, with *Velvet* lin'd.

The Royal MOURNER.

Upon the Princef Elizabeth's *Death.* 1652.

NO *Prophet's* tongue fhould this fad lofs condole,
  Unlefs firft heated by the *Altar's* coal.
Nor *Poet* to an *Elegy* afpire.
If not inlightn'd with *Apollo's* fire.

But yet my *Zeal* is warmer than his flame,
And I more nobly influenc'd by her *Name* ;
How, with more joy, had I imploy'd my hours
In writing of her *Sun-shine,* than her *showers?*
Ah! who would think such *Sun-beams* should be known
To dry all *Springs* of tears, unless her own ?
Or rather, that her *Suns,* (with all their beams)
Should be extinguish't by those native streams?
When the *World's Eye* its proper safety found,
And yet its *Body* was i' th' *Deluge* drown'd ;
With quickning smiles it did recruit the *Earth,*
Making it pregnant with a second birth ;
But hers (like *Nature* in her last extremes)
Melted a way, by weeping down their beams.
Such dashing rains, and Tempests often rage
I' th' *Winter Solstice* of afflicted age.
Experience then of woes occasion brings
To ope the *Flood-gates* of our flowing *Springs.*
Wet seed-times oft' are crown'd with *fruitful years* ;
And they shall reap in *joy* that sow in *tears.*
Her highest *Region* was free from the powers
Either of *sighing* storms, or *weeping showers.*
Like pow'rfull *Cynthia,* there her Soul did show,
Ruling the *Tides* of raging *Seas* below.
For she (like *Venus*) amidst *Seas* was born ;
And her short life, alas, one *rainy morn* !
Thus early *Lillies* (*Virgins* of the *year*)
Ne'r ope their wakeful *Eyes,* without a *tear.*
Too moist a *Season* makes 'em droop and dye,
And in their native *winding-sheets* to lie.
A common grief may common tears extort ;
But hers were *blood-drops* of a *weeping heart.*

Those

Those *Rubies* from her dying *Father's Head*,
Were not more fatal, than the tears she bled.
Thus *Flora's* justest Pride, the Rose, appears,
Produc'd not only, but nurst up with *Tears*.
All its short time with the like *drops* 'tis fed,
And tears each Night bedews its *fragrant* Bed.
At last, being tortur'd by *unnat'ral heats*,
Dyes as 'twas born, and weeps away in *Sweats*.

The Good BISHOP.

Upon Bishop Hall's *Balm of* Gilead, *presented to my
Uncle* Mr. Griff. Divall, 1652.

AGainst the pains, and multitude of cares
That bring on age, and Silver all our hairs
By *Nature's Chymistry* ; no means can add
More help, than *Hall's* rich *Balm of* Gilead.
Other old men, like common *Trees* do bear;   * Call'd the
He's fruitful (like that rare one)*twice a year.   Duce An.
All others blossom in the Spring; but he   ‖ As the
In Winter too, like th' ‖ *Glassenbury* tree.   Monks fa-
Winter yields Fruit; and in himself he shows   ble one did
The place where all the year an *Harvest* grows.   there eve-
His Judgment's brighter than the Sun's uprise ;   ry Christ-
Yet scorns to hide it self in *Evening-skies*.   mas-day,
Unchaste, intemp'rate Youth not seldom meets   as well as
An aged *Penance* nightly in the Sheets.   in May.
Lameness crawls after *Lust*; *Disease*, and *Pain*
Are all the *Bed-fellows* that now remain.
Rottenness waits on *Lux'ry*; its perfumes
Are putrefied *Lungs*, its *Baths* are *Rhewms*.

He's

He's troubled with no *Rhewm* but that of's *Pen*;
Always o'rflowing, and yet full agen.
Whose Springs are rarer than the *Spaws*; wherein
You may wash off the *Leprosie* of *Sin*.
His *Ink's* a Medicine, if us'd betimes,
To cure the *Tetters* of our spreading *Crimes*.
His *Pen* dropt daily at the *Nose* indeed ;
But then each drop turn'd *Balm* of *Gilead*.
What are his Words ? To speak Diviner sense,
Angels blest Food distill'd to Eloquence.
Had then that || *Father* known so great a Light || S.Hieuom.
Would shine to make the World's last Evening bright;
Who wish'd h' had liv'd Christ in the Flesh to see,
And *Rome's* great Empire in its Majesty ;
And *Paul* i'th' Pulpit ; thus his wish had run,
Paul in the Morn, *Hall* in the Afternoon.

To Mr. T.S. The Tooth-ach cur'd. 1652.

OH, how it stings ! Peace *Gouty* Sir, you'r blest
In such a Pain, as forces you to rest.
Mistake not, Madam, *Child-birth* is a toy ;
Nay, by your longing for't, it seems a Joy.
Hanging it self is not so sad a thing ;
Else at the *Gallows* they would never sing. (tongue!
Blest they; whose Mouths hold nothing but their
'Tis this sure makes our Grannams live so long.
Thrice happy they, who are o'th' horned crew ;
They've but one row of teeth, and full enow.
If *Cuckolds* had that priviledge by right,
I'd have a Wife my self before 'twas night.

Now

Now *Ælia's* Fate I wish, which I did flout,
Who with two coughs blew all her tushes out.
I sadly find their reason is not bad,
Who hold 'tis *Tooth-ach* makes our *Dogs* run mad.
Tormented still ! no ease ? pray, let m' alone ;
I've try'd all Remedies I've heard, but one.
That is -- as *old-Wifes* say, in ancient time
They cur'd the *Tooth-ach* with some *Charms* in *rhyme*,
Divine *Apollo*, then vouchsafe me ease.
Wondrous effects of *Verse* ! my Pains now cease
Thanks, great *Apollo* ! thanks I I find it true,
Thou'rt *God of Poets*, and *Physitians* too.

The BEADES-MAN.

To M. J. T. *sending begging Verses.* 1652.

I Thank you for your *Rhymes* ; there cannot be
  A surer voucher of your Poverty.
Verse shews a swelling mind, but a lank *Purse* ;
This makes me answer you again in *Verse.*
But to the purpose, Sir ; alas ! my fate
Fits me to pity, not to help your State.
And pity, without help, is just as good
As *much-good-doe-you*, when a Man wants Food.
God-help-you will not doe ; 'tis of no force ;
Prayers can do much ; these are but Words of course :
A *civil no* : a skillful *Beggar* swore
That *godly-talkers* seldom help the Poor.
Alas ! I cannot help it, I use wit
Sometimes like you, to bribe a benefit.

So

So that to beg of me is but to call
For Alms, at th' door of some poor *Hospital :*
I'm but a *Beads-man,* of the better note ;
Like them in every thing, but *Beard* and *Coat.*

The SEAL. 1652. *To Fr. L. Esq ;*

THEIR costly pride I hate, who did invent
 These *Silver Seals* ; 'twere better they were spent
In Sprightly *Sack,* than commonly to hing
By th' neck, at some old-greasie *Purse's* string ;
Or chain'd to rusty Keys : thus *Vulcan* joyn'd
With *Venus,* and black thighs with snowy twin'd.
As odd a *Match,* as when our *Syres* convey
Soft *Silver Curls, to Beards of Iron-gray.*
Poyson, like *Hannibal,* in Rings we wear ;
And, like to *Anchorites,* our *Coffins* bear.
To set our selves i' th' *stocks* is an odd jest,
As to turn *Bayliffs,* and our selves arrest.
Seals are for nothing good but to convey
Our Land (that clog of rising Souls) away.
No feats of *Chymistry* like this are told.
Nor sooner drosly Earth can turn to Gold,

The PROMISE.

To F. L. Esq ; with Crashaw's *Poems.* 1653.

THESE as I promis'd, Sir, I send.
 'Tis the chief duty of a *Friend*
(If that great honour you'l allow)
To owe his Life, and pay his Vow.

He

He that to's *Promiſe* does not ſtand,
Is *Knave* and *Fool* under's own hand.
Yet 'tis not wiſdom to appear
In Rhyme, when witty *Craſhaw*'s near.
A *Fool* that talks in a wiſe throng,
Libels himſelf with his own tongue.
A *Face* with native blackneſs tann'd,
Dares not before a Beauty ſtand.
My Muſe is very black and low,
And yet not proud, as Proverbs go.
Nor, like the *Gallants* of her *Sex*,
Does ſhe at greater Beauties vex.
She does not with pale Envy frown,
Becauſe ſhe wears the worſer *Gown*.
Yet when her Service ſhe expreſſes
To you, ſhe'd wear her richeſt Dreſſes.
Alas! that makes her Wants ſeem more;
So *Beggars* richeſt *rags* are *poor*.

Forc'd ABSENCE. 1654. *To* T. H.

WHat keeps thee, *Tom*, from viſiting thy Friend?
I gheſs the cauſe, & doubt thou canſt not mend.
Thou art quite out of *Robes*, haſt no *cloaths* new,
But what thou vapourd'ſt with in fifty two.
Thou com'ſt far ſhort of *Horſes*; they appear
More modiſh, and their *coats* caſt twice a year.
But one whole week abſtain from tempting *Ale*;
'Twill be apparent by thy little *Stale*;
'Tis ten to one thy *Dad* will not deny
Any thing, if thou ask him not to dye.

And

And that he'll scarcely do, (his Conscience such)
Until thy *Trap-stick* turn unto a *Crutch.*
O! that thou hadst a conscientious *Father,*
Whose *Eyes* and *Beard* would kindly out together;
Whose watchful Providence such care would keep,
To die whilst thou hadst Moisture left to weep.
But if he rub on still a few more years,
Rhewm will have spent the Stock of all thy tears,
And *Coughs* so waste thy breath, all will be gone,
Not any left thee to create a *Groan.*

The SHOWER. 1653.

To Mrs. S. V. being in the Rain. raptim.

THus looks a *Sea-Nymph,* when she leaves
   Her *Bed,* and rises from the *Waves* :
Thus *Flowers* we in *Water* steep,
That so they may their freshness keep.
Your *Tresses* are like *Sol's* bright Rayes,
When he appears in rainy dayes.
Diana when she did appear
I' th' *Fonntain,* was not half so fair ;
Her ruddy *Cheeks* deserve a Scoff,
Although a *blush* did set 'em off.

The Short ENJOYMENT. 1653.

To the same.

HEnce flatt'ring Fate, with hypocritick wiles!
   Thou that didst cheat me with *Sardonic* smiles!

                   Didst

Didſt mount me to receive the greater Fall ?
And give me *Honey* thus to ſwallow *Gall* ?
Thou ſhewd'ſt a chearful Countenance, as they
Who laviſh Smiles, but Smiles that will betray.
Though one Look from her can inrich my fate,
There is no man but would increaſe his State.
Alas ! like *Sun-ſhine* ſeen in cloudy dayes,
I only ſaw a glimm'ring of her Rayes.
Fortune on ſome beſtowes a happy fate,
Only to make them more unfortunate.
Beaſts for the *Sacrifice* were crown'd with *Wreaths* ;
And ſometimes men are brisk before their deaths.
Deceiving *twilight* ! checquer'd with the powers
Of Light and Darkneſs ! thus the *April-ſhowers*
Drown'd the faint *Sun-beams* : *Midwives* daily try,
We're born no ſooner than have cauſe to cry.
Thus did I ſee her, but ſoon loſt her ſight ;
She, and the Sun withdraw their Beams at night.
She, like a fatal flaſh of *Lightning*, ſhin'd
With ſudden glance, only to ſtrike me blind.

The C O N V E Y A N C E. 1654.

To Mrs. S. V.

Madam,

MY thoughts were vain, as well as high,
   To hope the favour of your Eye.
You ſhed your Beams on Objects fine,
On ſuch as do deſerve your ſhine.
Your Rayes live at a higher rate
Than *Sol's* ; who does debaſe his State

In gilding Dirt ; all muſt confeſs,
In ſeeing us, you do no leſs.

   Yet, ſince we Ruſticks juſtly may,
In Harveſt, wiſh a Sun-ſhine day ;
'Tis not a crime to wiſh you here ;
For without you no dayes are clear.
This *Paper* rhymes, -- becauſe 'tis meet
A *Lacquey* ſhould not want his *feet* :
Such is my *Muſe*; who comes to day,
Only this Letter to convey.
Acceptance almoſt is its due ;
Since, *Madam*, it was born for you.
'Twill ne'r appear, unleſs it be
Adorn'd in your rich *Livery.*
For *Wit* and *Fancy* grow ſo ſcarce,
Your *Name* muſt bring 'em into *Verſe.*

The F R O S T. 1654. *To Mr.* W. L.

THE *ſtreams* are *fetter'd*, and with us as rare,
   As *Fountains* in *Arabian Deſarts* are.
No tears in *Woman's* Eyes ; their skill is croſt,
And that moſt ready *Fountain* now is loſt.
Our *Noſe-drops* freez to Pearls, and *Jewels* there,
Like ſalvage *Indians*, we are forc'd to wear.
Bracelets may now be cheap ; our *Laſſes* try --
They can ſpit forth as good as they can buy.
Glaſs-Fornaces are needleſs ; he's an Aſs
That will buy any, when he piſſes *Glaſs*,
Surgeons, with all their Lancets, do no good ;
Our Veins are ſtufft with *Coral*, not with *Blood.*

                                  To

To be i' th' Rain the *Service* now's as hot,
As 'twixt two *Armies* joyn'd ; each *drop's* a *shot*.
Each *Hail* a *Bullet*, shot with ratling noise ;
And *Snow* (*white-Powder*) silently destroys,
If now our *sheep* lye down upon the Grass, || Plant-Ani-
You'd swear how each a || *Boronetho* was,   mal.
And there took rooting : for thus fixt they show
Like snowy *Hillocks*, or like breathing *Snow*.
Fish freeze i' th' *Deeps*, and think't a happy lot
Now to be caught and put into a *Pot*.
And *Hares* ev'n frozen in their *Forms* do lye,
As they had put themselves into a *Pye*

    Nature's inslav'd ; her very Breath confin'd,
Her *Lungs* are stopt, and cannot gather Wind.
Sometimes she's raging mad, and fiercely blows,
Foaming and *Froathing* all the *Earth* with *Snows*.
Those downy *show'rs* appear (which *Boreas* brings)
As though the *moulting* Clouds had *mew'd* their *wings* ;
What else is *Snow* but *feather'd drizzel*, blown
Fro' th' Sky, where their swift *Pinnions* late had flown ;
No other *flights* than these now haunt the Air,
Till *lym'd* with *frost*, they're forc'd to tarry here.

    The *Air's* so thick it does like th' *Dead-Sea* flow
Where *Birds*, with *feather'd Odrs*, can scarcely row.
And hollow *Clouds*, ramm'd full as they can bear,
Discharge *Hail-shot* in *Volleys* through the Air.
Those *Dew-drops* that upon the Earth are found,
Right *Pearls* they are, and pave the glitt'ring ground.
Wherever any graffy *Turf* is view'd,
It seems a *Tansie* all with *Sugar* strew'd.

    The Sea is one *great Blister*, till the Sun
Pierce the *thick skin* and make the *Water* run.

             C   'Twas

'Twas ne'r the Sun's right *Looking-Glass* before ;
Ice is the *Chryftal*, lin'd with *filver Oar*.

    Bold Briitain (if but to her felf a Friend)
All the World elfe feeks vainly her t' offend.
Safe-bulwarkt with *two Walls* that fates do grant ;
With thofe of *Wood* and thefe of *Adamant*.

    Ladies now teftifie what Poets told ;
True *Pearls* they weep, *Silver* they void and *Gold* ;
But, ah ! for all thefe Comforts they are cold !
We *Men* grow *ftiff* ! no punifhment is worfe,
When former bleffings turn a horrid curfe.
Love cools ; nay burning *Luft* is frozen *dead*,
As cooling *Metals* lofe their fhining *Red*.
The *Nuptial fheets* ev'n freez into a *Tomb* ;
And *Lovers*, their own *ftatues* there become.
If fome fmall *Thaw* from *Nature*'s warmth appears,
The *aid* is *comfortlefs* that ends in *Tears*.

The S H R Y N E. 1665.

Upon feeing her in a Scarlet-Velvet-Mantle.

AUrora thus begins to rife,
    When fhe with *Crimfon* trims the Skies ;
But her weak beams are conquer'd foon ;
Yours, *Madam*, triumph o're the Sun.
Too fiercely they our Eyes affail'd,
If *Mofes*-like you were not veild.
Infolded there, your fweets make good,
You are a *Damask-Rofe* i' th' *bud*.
Rofes, when they lay by their leaves,
(Thofe *Velvet-Mantles Nature* gives)

Lolo

Lose their chief Vertue ; all confess,
You are most sweet without your Dress.
Yet since we use with reverence,
A *Carkass,* when the *Soul's* flown thence ;
And when obedience here was shown,
They honour'd *Courts,* though *Kings* were gone ;
Let us, when we her presence want,
Adore the *Shrine* that held the *Saint.*
Divines affirm our *Churches* are
Sacred for th' *Service* offer'd there.
Rich *Mantle!* when thou her dost fold,
Thou art the *Mine,* and she the *Gold.*
Nature's Exchequer, where does lye
The total of her Treasury.
The *Zodiac* never did intwine
More Beauties, than are clos'd in thine,
From her it takes the dazling Grace :
The *Sun-beams* shine so through a Glass.
Thus the expanded Chrystal Skies,
That both inlight, and bless our Eyes ;
Yet serve but as a glorious Skreen,
For greater beauties are within.
Nor is it vain to praise the *Shell,*
And not the *Pearl* that there does dwell ;
It is enough, if here my Muse
Can do, but as our *Ladies* use,
When they on *Limons* set their minds,
And only Candy o're the *Rinds.*

The KISS. 1656. *To Mrs.* C.

HOLD not your Lips fo clofe; difpence
   Treafures, Perfumes, and Life from thence.
Squeeze not thofe full-ripe *Cherries*; this
Becomes a *Simper*, not a *Kifs*.
There's danger to lock up your Breath,
It *Coufin-German* is to *Death*.
None *baggs* up wind, the *Merchant* fwears,
Unlefs fome wrinkled *Laplanders*.
What needs this Guard ; it is fmall fence
Thus to hedge in a double *Fence*.
Clos'd Lips exprefs but filent Bliffes,
And at the beft are but dumb *Kiffes*.
You are with *Cupid* little kind,
To make him *Dumb* as well as *Blind*.
Such *Smacks* but fhew a filent ftate ;
Kiffes fhould be articulate.
An *open-mouthed* Kifs fpeaks fence,
It is the Lovers eloquence,
Let yours fpeak out then ; there's no Blifs
To th' *Pronuntiation* of a *Kifs*.

The SCANDAL. 1656.

Upon Mrs. K. C. *raifing one.*

HOW now, mad *Kitling*, peevifh *Brat* !
   Canft thou no fooner fee, than fcrat ?
That all who fee thee, juftly doubt
Alecto in her *Swathing-clout*.

Feat early Mifchief! tell me why
Thou fought'ft to wound me with this lie?
What's my offence? is it not this,
Becaufe I do no oftner kifs ?
What Fool would do himfelf the wrong,
To venture half fo near thy *Tongue?*
Far worfe than *Snakes,* or *Adders* are ;
Thou dangers doft at both ends bear.
Thou'rt worfe than *Scorpions,* who bring
A cure themfelves for thofe they fting.
But thou'rt all o're with *Venom* fmear'd ;
Thy very *Looks* are to be fear'd ;
Not that thy *Glances* have a fpice
Of *Venus,* but of *Cockatrice.*
Nor boaft thy *Flaxen Curls* ; they be
As well figns of a *Leprofie.*
That *Rock of Tow* upon thy *Head,*
Prove there are *Poyfon-pates,* not *Red.*

The Vertues of C A N A R Y. 1656.

Tune Ifaac's Balls. To Mr. G. H.

S'Ack will make a *Coward* Fight,
    And his Humour vary ;
It will infufe a Nobler Sp'rite,
    Than great *Hector's* did carry :
    Nay it fo will play its part,
He had rather fpill a *Quart*
Of *Blood,* than of *Canary.*

Sack makes the daring *Seaman* wife,
    And refolute as *Phocion* ;

Not all the *Artillery* of the *Skies*,
Can make him alter his brave motion;
Tho' *Tempests* rage, and *Thunder* crack,
    Let him be drowned first in *Sack*,
And a *Fico* for the *Ocean.*

If you would have a *Doctor* wife,
    Bestow on him a *Pottle.*
All *Wisdom* in the *Bottom* lies,
No *Helicon* unto the *Bottle.*
And when he can pour down no more,
He will upon his Knees adore
    Bacchus, above *Aristotle.*

Sack can make an *Alderman* wife,
    And venture at a Ditty:
'Twill make a *Beggar's* thoughts to rise
    Let his shirt be ne'r so Nitty.
It can make sweet the crabbed face
Of *Sergeants,* and coutroul their *Mace,*
    And melt the *Rogues* to pitty.

If one have but a spark of Wit,
    Sack will quickly show it;
And in troth I think it fit,
    By my example you should know it;
For, as once my *Lord Gray* said,
I this fine new-sing-song made,
But *Sack* made me the *Poet.*

Th

P O E M S. 23

The DELUGE. 1657.
Upon the Death of R. Sanderſon *Eſq* ;
by the Eruption of a Vein.

SAD *Deluge,* this ! what could no Art reſtrain,
Nor ſtop th' o'rflowing *Chanal* of a Vein ?
A *Flood* in *Harveſt* thus deſtroys the hopes
Of all the Year, and ſpoils the fruitful Crops.
Bleſt Nilus ! thou deſerv'ſt immortal thanks ;
Thou profit bring'ſt, when thou o'rflow'ſt thy *Banks.*
Of all ſad *Deluges* this was the worſt,
And little leſs deſtructive than the *firſt.*
Where's *Surgery* become, that boaſted Theme ?
No *Sluce,* no *Flood-gate* that can turn this *Stream* ?
Shall the dull *Dutch* damm up the Springs o'th' Sea,
And fetter *Neptune,* till his *Tides* obey ?
Yet our fam'd *Artiſts* ſtudy all in vain
To ſtop the little Torrent of a Vein ?
Let us confide no more in erring *Duſt* ;
That great *Phyſician* may command our Truſt,
Who ſtopt, by touching of his *Garment*'s hem,
Th' unruly Current of a Bloody *Stream.*
Nay more ; by vertue of his ſole command,
And ſacred Pow'r allow'd to *Moſes*'s *Wand,*
Stop't the *Red-Sea,* and check'd the foaming Tide,
Roaring and ſwelling with impetuous pride :
And made the crouding Waves, on either hand,
Like ſhining Walls of poliſh'd *Chryſtal* ſtand ;
He ! he alone ! ſuch Miracles can ſhow,
And ſtop thoſe *Fountains* who firſt made 'em *flow.*

C 4   The

The RECOVERY. 1657
To my dear S. Mrs. S. S.

SO you recruit, tell me no more
  Of leſſer beauty than before ;
Yet where's the loſs ? ſince ſtill I'ſpy
Thoſe Arched Brows, that ſparkling Eye.
Wherein ſuch contradiction fix,
That *Sun* and *Clouds* together mix.
Though neither conquer, yet both fight ;
No *Cloud* ſo black, no *Sun* ſo bright.
A *Sun* with no *Eclipſes* harm'd :
A *Cloud* with *Lightning* ever arm'd :
Then is not here each charming grace
That formerly ſhin'd in that *Face ?*
Thoſe modeſt ſmiles, whoſe native flight
At once denies, yet does invite ?
Like a *Gilt-harneſt-valiant Foe,*
Whoſe *Arms* cry, *Take me, Sword* ſays *no.*
What *Parts* then do theſe wants diſcloſe ?
Becauſe each *Cheek* has loſt its *Roſe,*
Your *Lips* their Cherries ? never fear ;
Tho' th' *Seaſon*'s paſt, they'l ſpring next year.
Your *Sickneſs* did this *Autumn* bring ;
But *Health* will ſoon create a *Spring.*

The POET. 1657.

Upon that incomparable Enthuſiaſt
Mr. Jo. Cleveland.

WHo'ere reads *Cleveland* (*Leader* of the *Pack*)
  Carouzes Eſſences, and ſp'rit of *Sack.*

                              For

For what he drank, it was for publick ufe ;
And, in his Brains, he did preferve the *Juyce.*
Where heated in his Head (that *Chymic Still*)
Wits-Effence flow'd fro' th' Spout of his rich *Quill.*
The *Sun* thus moifture fucks, and after pours
From *cloudy Limbecks* all the fruitful fhowers.
His *wit* was univerfal : like the Sun,
It gilded every thing it look'd upon.
Some (as poor I) rich Subjects do debafe ;
He (like great *Monarchs*) did the pooreft grace:
By his rare faculty our Times were mov'd
To think that barren *Forefts* might b' improv'd.
Each matter hits aright to his defire ;
His conqu'ring flame converted all to fire.
The higheft things did to his fancy ftoop ;
The *Scythian* fo proud *Bajazet* did coop.
His *wit* was free, not to *fet-rules* confin'd ;
But clear, and ripening like the *Summer-Wind.*
Pleafure and profit he from thence did bring ;
As it makes *Corn* to grow, and *Flowers* to fpring.
He made the *Company* where 'ere he came ;
And warm'd the coolnefs, or elfe quencht the flame.
Nor did he owe one help to any man,
Like thofe firft *Heroes* who all *Arts* began.
His thriving thoughts no Foreign Aids did need,
But on their fruitful *Soyl* alone did feed.
He ne'r the way of our new *Rhymers* chofe,
In *racking,* or (at beft) *Tranflating* profe.
To force his *Fancy* he did never ufe,
Like fome who ravifh an unwilling *Mufe,*
Was big with thought, yet happy in his choice,
Like the fmooth'd tuning of a *nat'ral Voice.*

The

The *Subject* known, he did the *humours* hit;
First chose the *stuff*, then did the *Ribbons* fit.
His *Fancies* jostled, were together prest;
Puzzled he was to chuse, not make the best.
His *Refuse* would inrich us all; the poor
Thrive thus by raking at the rich Man's door.
He was more than us all! Imagine what
He could say of himself, and *Cleveland's* that.

DISCREET LOVE. 1657. To M. S.

PEace, *Syrens*, Peace! experienc'd harms
    Serve but to antidate your Charms.
The *World's* more wise now, than to seek
Roses and *Lillies* in a *Cheek*;
Coral in *Lips*; himself he mocks
That looks for *Sun-beams* in her *Locks*.
Or he who fancies those blew stains
Saphyres or *Violets*, but *Veins*.
None trusts an amorous Muse, that sings
His *Mistress Breasts* two *Nectar springs*,
Lockt up with *Rubies*, that there grow,
Soft *Marble Quarries*, and warm *Snow*;
That she sweats *Amber*, breaths sweet *Gums*,
Voids *Marmalad*, and vents *Perfumes*.
Beauty's the Sawce, that brings delight
To *Love*, which is the *Appetite*:
But *Wealth's* the *Food*; 'tis a sad pause,
When hungry, to have only *Sawce*:
Thus foolish Boys neglect their meat,
So they may *red-cheek'd Apples* eat.

Beauty

Beauty is only in the *Skin* ;
The worth, and fubftance is within ;
'Tis fpoil'd when us'd ; now *Gold's* more bright
With time, and ufe ; *Aurora's* light
Improves thus till the *Sun* does rife ;
(That *twenty-fhillings-piece* o' th' *skies*)
Talk then no more of loving faces,
Of outward parts, and inward graces ;
Since *Cupid's* felf can ftrike no heart
In love, without his *golden dart.*

The Refolute CO URTIER.   1658.

PRethee fay I or no ;
   If thou't not have me tell me fo,
         I cannot ftay ;
         Nor will I wait upon
         A fmile, or frown.
         If thou wilt have me fay ;
Then I am thine, or elfe I am mine own.

         Be white or black ; I hate
Dependence on a checker'd fate,
         Let go, or hold ;
         Come either kifs or not ;
         Now to be hot,
         And then again as cold,
Is a fantaftick Fever you have got.

A te-

A tedious Wooe is bafe,
And worfe by far than a long Grace :
For whilft we ftay,
Our lingring fpoils the Roaft,
Or Stomach's loft ;
Nor can, nor will I ftay;
For if I fup not quickly, I will faft.

Whilft we are frefh, and ftout,
And vigorous, let us to't :
Alas, what good
From wrinkled Man appears,
Gelded with years ;
When his thin wheyifh Blood,
Is far lefs comfortable than his Tears.

Right COURTSHIP. 1658.

SHould I kifs every one that's fair,
    Or marry all I court ;
I like the *Captain* fhould appear,
    That conquered every *Fort*,
And nothing left for thofe that love the *Sport*.

What matter I though *Rumour* fnarle,
    That I took not the *Town* :
Since I did bring her to a *Parle*,
    It is as much renown,
As If I knock'd, and beat her *Bulwarks* down.

Self-

Self-int'reſt is the ſafeſt claim,
    Let *Wealth*, and *Worth* be had;
To level there's the ſureſt aim,
    And he the wiſeſt *Lad*.
Who makes no *Match*, but by a *Match* is made.

The P L A G I A R Y. 1658.

Upon S.C. *a* Presbyterian *Miniſter, and Captain,
ſtealing* 48 *Lines from* Craſhaw's *Poems
to patch up an* Elegy *for Mr.* F. P.

MOnſtrous! and Strange! & ſcarcely heard of yet!
    A *Presbyterian*, and pretend to wit!
Steel'd arrogance! to nibble at the crime
Of *Verſe*, and meddle with that *Dagon-Rhyme*!
Tremble, great *Dogril Sir*, at what I ſay;
For *Verſe* is *Couſin German* to a *Play*..
But *Poets* may' with *Church-men* well agree:
David did *Verſes* make, and *Prophecie*.
This is his canting Plea; but ſoft, Sir, ſtand;
You are arraign'd for Theft, hold up your hand.
Impudent Theft, as ever was expreſt,
Not to ſteal Jewels only, but the Cheſt.
Not to nib bits of *Gold* from *Craſhaw's* Lines,
But ſwoop whole Strikes together from his *Mynes*!
Unconſcionable thief ! than * *Hind* far worſe;   * A famous
To rob one both of *Money* and of *Purſe*.   Robber.
Thou, of thy *Brethren-Taxers*, get'ſt the ſtart,
In taking more than th' *five and twentieth part*:
Like to thoſe *Fiends* we *Sequeſtrators* call,
Thy ſtretching Conſcience goes away with all.

Arch

Arch piece of *Robbery! Gigantick* knack !
To take both *Goods* and *House* too on thy back;
Quote *Scripture* for't, as for *Rebellion,* fay,
Sampfon in *Gaza* took the *Gates* away.
Thy *Mufe, Philira* like, is turn'd a *Mare*;
And by his *Pegafus* is cover'd here.
Unnat'ral *Coupling* this as e're did pafs;
As if his *Pegafus* fhould *leap* an *Afs!*
Like a *Drum-major,* he with Zeal appears,
Beating his *Pulpit* to get *Volunteers.*
Thy *Black-coat,* furious *Jehu,* moft men think
Takes colour from thy *Powder,* not thine *Ink*;
And thy *Dragooning Genius* has a fhare
More in *Salt-peter* than Saint *Peter's Chair.*
How much the *Caufe* owes to this *Braves* command,
Who taught *Rebellion* both with *Tongue* and *Hand*;
As *Balaam* of his *Afs,* he learnt this Trick
Of fome fuch *Colt,* both for to *whee* and *kick.*
A *Preacher! Captain, Thief,* and *Poet* view!
A *Jack* of all *Trades,* and of all *Sides* too.
But *Mar-text,* how doft thou declare thine hate,
In joyning *Poets* with the *Bifhops* Fate?
To rail at *Poets,* but to fteal their *ftrains,*
To hate the *Bifhops,* but to love their *means.*
Did parted Souls (as fome have held) but know
Thofe things are done by their left friends below ;
Think'ft thou deceafed *Pierpont* likes fuch *Verfe*
As thou haft filch'd here to adorn his *Herfe?*
Judge but how fuch an Act thy felf would fcan,
A *Thief* fubfcribe thee for an *Honeft Man,*

The OLD MAN. 1658.

An Epitaph upon my Gr. Mr. T. S.

HERE lies an aged *Corps*, which late
   Incag'd a *Soul* ; whom neither fate,
Nor Times, could change from its firſt State.

Oppreſt more with Age than cares :
Reſpected more for *Silver hairs*
Than *Gold* ; for Wiſdom more than Years.

Happy in every *Child* he had ;
Happy in ſelf, and only ſad,
Being born in good days, but deceas'd in bad.

The MOURNER. 1659.

Upon the Death of my dear Father, Mr. W. S.

LET not the ranting Crew explode my Tears ;
   Nor ſtop my ſighings with their Mocks and Jeers :
Such as lament in *Sack* for Father's dying,
'Till Eyes look red, then ſwear it came with crying :
Who to the *Church* ſuch modiſh *Mourners* come,
As if they meant to revel o're the Tomb.
I leave that road, ſo that I now forbear
To ſtrew his Grave, but with a gaudy tear.
For Drops of Ink are ſo that do diſtill
From a luxuriant, or too trim a Quill.
Nor let ſome think the grief is ſmall, where time,
And ſuch Compoſure is to build a *Rhyme*

                  Since

Since *David's Muse* did never higher rife,
Than when it took its fountain from his *Eyes:*
And if in thefe *Lines* any Life can be,
Or can tranfmit it to *Pofterity* ;
'Tis but a juft endeavour *Life* to give
To that lov'd Perfon, who did make me live.
Not that I think this power in my *Verfe*,
(The common *Hatchment* now of every Herfe)
But in his Vertues, which they would declare;
Thefe give the life of which thofe hope a fhare.
For thus a *Pen* that limms a good man's ftory,
Improves its own, well as the fubjects glory.
So every *Duty* is a Benefit,
And gains a bleft reward for doing it,
I wifh I could his Vertues imitate,
And praife together ; fuch a lucky fate
Befell that *Orator*, who as he ftood
Praifing his vertuous Friend, himfelf turn'd good.

His Zeal to *God* and *Church* glow'd with that heat
Firft *Chriftians* us'd, without the modern cheat.
* Loyal to's *Prince* without the hope of gains,
And conftant too in midft of lofs and chains.
His Prayers were fervent, and his Faith was ftrong,
Still hop'd, although *Rebellion* profper'd long.
At length the ftorm blew o're, the skyes did clear,
And light begun to gild our *Hemifphere.*
His breaft with publick joy fo over-flow'd,   * Imprifoned
His Soul was forc'd to leave its old aboad :   long by the
                                                  Rebels at *Not-*
Yet like the *dying Swan* he tun'd his knell,   *tingham. vid.*
And with old *Simeon* fung his own *farewell.*

Thus

Thus the long look'd-for *Prospect Moses* gain'd;
He faw, but ne're injoy'd the *Promis'd Land.*

Wit's E P I C E D I U M. 1659.
Epitaph upon Mr. J. Cleveland.

HERE lies great *Cleveland* ! whom 'tis fit,
To name the *Phœnix* of true Wit.
His *Fate* fuits fadly with the name ;
Since he expired in a *Flame.*
A *Fever* ! hence this fate did come,
The *Mufes* fuffer'd *Martyrdom*!
He like the *Phœnix* dy'd ! Alas !
Not like the *Phœnix* bury'd was!
Since with the *Gums* of his own *Stile*,
He did not build himfelf a *Pyle.*

The D I V I N E. 1659.
Upon Dr. Huit's *Death by* Cromwel.

RAfh times, and men, to hurry hence
What Ages cannot recompence !
For by his timelefs death we loft
The rarities of holy coft.
He try'd all *Learning*, and from thence
Did cull the perfect quintefcence
Hence was his *Tongue* with Effence tipt,
His *Lips* in heavenly *Nectar* dipt.
He pleas'd the Mind, and eas'd the Heart ;
His *Sermons* twifted Grace and Art.
His *Zeal* was learn'd he could intice
A man, with pleafure, from a Vice,

D   Thofe

Those who did hear his *Sermons* right,
And practis'd, grew good with delight;
He heard his *Sentence* with that chear,
That upstart *Lords their Titles* hear.
Let *Traitors* quake with crimes opprest;
Let guilt raise *Earthquakes* in their Breasts;
Let a rebellious *Ague* seize
Their bloods, and Horrour turn disease;
Let such ones tremble : Glorious Soul *!*
Thou dost thine envious fate controul:
What Coward arm'd with thy sure Ward,
Need fear a *Tower* or a *Guard* ?
Halbards and *Troops* (ta'n in right sence)
Serv'd but to guard thine Innocence.
Thy *Cause*, and *Spirit* makes us vow
Thy *Judges* suffer'd, and not thou.
Their bloody *Sentence* (to their spight)
More then their *Pardon*, did thee right;
The *Axe* cut them; and once they'l know
They had by far the worser blow.
Thy rising Soul was then more tall,
When others stoop, just at thy fall;
Sol biggest is, when he does come
To rest thus in his *Western* home;
In *Seas* he sets, and thou in *tears*;
Thine *Ocean* far more deep appears.
And when thou dost in Glory rise,
Thy beams will daze their blood-shot-*Eyes.*

The

The A D A M I T E. 1659.

Upon the loſs of a Ladies Linnens ; all her Shifts
and Cloaths being ſtollen.

A *Dam* of temper'd *Clay* was rais'd ;
  His *Body* with rich *Linnen* cas'd ;
An earthen *Veſſel* finely glas'd.

But *Eve* was of a purer frame ;
She from compleated *Adam* came :
From the young *Sun* ſo ſhin'd the *Flame.*

To him ſhe ſeem'd a glorious ſight ;
Her very *Nakedneſs* was bright :
Thus is the *Moon skin'd* o're with light.

Her *Innocence* no *Coverings* had ;
'Twas *Guilt* did cauſe the *Fig-leaf* ſhade :
As *Beams* are hid by *Clouds* they made.

Beſides, the *Spring-time* now invites
Nature, to bleſs our wondring ſights.
With her rare *Cloſet* of Delights.

Lillies (thoſe *Virgins* of the year)
Their Snowy *Boſoms* now appear ;
Each opening her lac'd *Stomacher.*

Tulips ſtart from their *Winter-beds,*
Unfolding their thick *Coverlids* ;
Lie bare, and ſhew their *Maiden-heads.*

Roſes

Roses although with blushes born,
Their *green-silk Plackets* now are torn,
And shew their beauties to the *Morn*.

Your *Hand* faire *Lady*, then hold by,
Or kindly let my searching Eye
Through th' *Lattice* of your *Fingers* pry.

The *Russian Empress* need not fear,
If Cold or shame would *Coverings* wear,   * A rich sort
She's cloath'd with native * *Miniver*   of Furr.

The A R C H-T R A I T O R. 1659.

Upon the Death of Oliver Cromwell.

THE *Muses*, like the *Cavaleers*, confin'd,
    (For *Wit* and *Loyalty* are best, when joyn'd)
Have now their liberty : the time affords
Poets to use their *Pens*, and those their *Swords* :
The *Tyrant* knew by both he might be harm'd ;
So *Playes* he voted down, and them disarm'd.
For he did doubt whether more hurt might rise,
Or from the *Standish*, or the *Mortar-piece*.
Arm'd against *Swords*, but not 'gainst *Cleveland*'s *Quill*
More sharp than *Porcupines*, it pierc'd his *Steel*.
Twas try'd of old when feather'd *Arrows* flew,
They far more *Foes* than all our *Cannons*, slew.
'Twas this made him so cautiously severe ;
Poets and *Souldiers* tam'd, he did not fear.
But all his cruel Policies were vain ;
Mastiffs are much the fiercer for the *Chain*.

Helicon

Helicon rougher runs when'tis difturb'd,
And *Pegafus* kicks more for being curb'd.
Who did his *Provant,* and his *Curb* neglect ;
Nor would thofe clear *Streams* his grim looks reflect.
'Tis true, a *Slave* or two, to fhew his face, Let fome of
Made *Stix,* not *Helicon* his *Looking-Glafs.* our fam'd Po-
Their *Turkifh* Souls and fancies were fo vain ets and their
To ferve as *Footftools* to that *Tamberlane.* be here exa-
Their mercenary *Bays* as largely fpread mined.
Upon the *Tyrant's* as the *Prince's* head. One noted
Bafe! that in verfe *Rebellion* fhould appear; Poet, his Pane-
As though *Apollo* were turn'd *Presbyter.* gyrtck upon *O-*
liver.
As th' *Mufes* (ftirred up by zealous wrath)
Should lend their *Treafures* to the *Publick Faith.*
Wretches ! who if they live to better days,
May merit Hempen Wreaths, inftead of Bayes.
Wit, like true Courage, never fhould abate,
But bravely ftand unmov'd in fpite of Fate;
Confront the *Tyrant* in his guarded *Den,*
And, like bold *Brutus,* ftab him with a *Pen.* *He fir'd it, and
then laid it on
the *Chriftians.*
* *Nero* fet *Rome* on fire, a crime Severe !
Noll fir'd three Kingdoms, and then warm'd him there ;
Play'd o're the Flames, and long exulting ftood ;
Then ftrove to quench them with the Natives blood.

Nor was't enough to make our *Purfes* pay ;
But *Taxes* on our *Confciences* to lay.
We might connive not only at his Guilt,
But take on us the blood the *Tyrant* fpilt.
The *Commons* did it ; he like *Pilate,* ftands ;
And we the Water hold to wafh his hands.

Pro-

Prodigious arrogance ! he did defie
The chiefeft pow'rs both of the Earth and Sky !
Againft both God, and Church he ftood alone;
Thruft one fro'th' Church, the other from the Throne.
His facrilegious hands at once pluck'd down
The facred *Myter,* and the regal *Crown.*
The *Graces,* and the *Mufes* he accus'd
Becaufe by's luft they would not be abus'd.
And yet this devillifh *Hypocrite* would pray,
Hyena like would cry, and then betray.
With counterfeiting groans he hid his wiles,
Like to the treacherous fobs of *Crocodiles.*
His Tears, like thofe of *baneful Yew* did trill,
Whofe baneful drops their neighb'ring Trees do kill.
His *whining* always did portend fome harm:
So hardeft *Marbles* weep againft a Storm.
His *Trulyes* cheated, and his *Smiles* betray'd ;
In *Velvet-skabbard* lay his *murd'ring* blade.
His poys'nous heart in *Beds of Flowers* lay ;
Like *Quagmires* into which their *Greens* betray.
A *Sodom-Apple,* rotten at the *Coar* ;
A *Peftilential Bubo* plaifter'd o're.
But now the *Botch* is broke ; his Reign is done,
And he himfelf into *Corruption* run.

The APPARITION. 1659.
Upon Cromwel's *burying (by* Ireton) *in* Weft-
minfter Abby.

PArdon, great Souls, if I prefume
So near, as your *Withdrawing room* ;

You

Your royal *Wardrobe,* wherein rests
Your *Garniture* in *Marble Chests.*
Safely lockt up, to make more gay
Your second *Coronation* day.
Then will those *mouldy Garments* shine
Like that pure *stuff,* which them must line.
Air'd by the influence of a *Ray,*
Stronger then what gives life to *Day.*
Which will new cloath that *Beldame Night*
With robes, spun of eternal light.
Will make the Sun in *Cynders* lye ;
That *Phœnix* in its Nest to dye.
For it would be a needless sight,
When every object is more bright.
That shining time we once must know :
Ift be allow'd to call it so,
When no degree nor space is found,
But an immortal *Nunc* goes round.
This thought such deep impressions makes
My muse with awful rev'rence shakes.
Methinks I hear the *Trumpet*'s sound ;
An *Earth-quake* strikes the palsy'd ground.
The *Marbles* now discharge their trust,
And faithfully return their *Dust.*
Behold the quickning *Attoms* play,
Invited by an heavenly ray.
In close embraces dancing round,
'Till each its old position found,
Uniting then with joy, they rest ;
Form'd to a *Temple* fitly drest
To hold the *bright descending Guest.*

Who

Who will not lofe by changing place,
Convey'd into its fhining *Cafe* ;
As *Sun-beames* into *Chryftal* pafs.
Thus animated from above,
Look how the *rifing Monarchs* move !
With *lofty meen* they Earth defpife ;
|| *Gods now indeed*, and worthy Skies !
Attended by a fitting Train,
Which humbly at their feet had lain.
No Subject boafts a nobler ftate,
Than on his *Prince's duft* to wait.
Kings honour bring where they refort,
Making ev'n *Golgotha* a *Court*.

> || Kings are efteem'd Gods, but dye like men.

    From Heav'n amongft the Angels came
A glitt'ring *Wayter* called *Fame* ;
Breaking her *Trumpet* with a blaft;
For what needs *Fame* when time is paft ?
Here other *Heralds* then appear'd,
Thofe *Poets* that were there interr'd :
'Tis fit they fhould fome glory fhare,
Who did fo much advance it here.

    Juft as all thefe prepar'd to fly
To the fhining *Rendezvous* i' th' Sky ;
Two *Monfters* from their *filth* did craul ;
Off'ring to rife, ftill down they fall.
Their *blood-fhot* eyes, with gloating fhame,
Too weak to bear the heavenly flame
Of fuch a *Prefence* dazling bright,
With glory crown'd and roab'd with light.
One of 'em with a glaring look,
Swelling with fpite, and fury fpoke.

"Thefe,

"Thefe are but *Kings*, and *Cromwell*, I !
"They at my *Genius* us'd to fly.
"*Death* (that great *Tyrant*) being dead;
"Why fhould we petty *Monarchs* dread ?
"What makes us fo dejected lie?
"Thofe vainly fear that cannot die.

"Yet die we will rather then fhun   } * That Villain
"To act what we before have done ;   } drew the Ar-
"Quoth damn'd remonftring * *Ireton.* } mies Remon-
"Let's charge their *Troop*, and both prepar'd,   ftrance, which
Red fury from their *Beacons* glar'd ;   was the mo-
Their heads the groveling ferpents rear'd.   ving caufe of
                                             the K I N G's
                                             Death.

--------Fame then reply'd-----

"Avaunt, thou odious fpawn of Night ;
" Thou *Beam* i' th' very Eye of Light !
"Wer't not enough you did defile
("Nay worfe, profan'd) this *hallow'd Soyle* ;
"Reducing it to fo vile price,
"Like *Egypt*'s it may turn to *Lice* ?
"Were't not enough you did invade
" Their Throne, but you ufurp their *Shade*?
" Purfuing them ev'n to the *Tombe*,
"And now dare in their *Prefence* come ?
" You ought to be (for this bold crime)
"Damn'd down to Hell before your time.

Like red-hot Iron then *Cromwel* glowes,
Yet nothing fhin'd unlefs his *Nofe*.

Of

Of red, and blew mixt was the flame ;
As it from *Fire* and *Brimstone* came.
The *Angel* shunning further stay,
His Heavenly Banner did display,
Such power i'th' sacred *Cross* did dwell ;
Struck with its Lightning, down they fell,
For ought I know, as deep as Hell.
Humbly the shining presence bow'd,
And *Hallelujahs* sung aloud.
All ravish'd with the heavenly noise.
Amaz'd I op'd my wondring Eyes.
When nothing did to them, alas, appear !
But all these *Glories* vanish'd into *Air*.

The A B S E N C E. 1660.

To Captain Ben. Marshal *leaving* Newark.

GOod-*Fellowship* begins to mourn,
And in thine absence, finds its *Urne*.
When now we meet, 'tis to condole
Our *Bodies* rob'd of thee, the *Soul*.
And since thou art from *Newark* fled,
Both *Sack* and *Ale* for grief are dead.
Thus standing *Brooks* begin to stink,
When *Sol* is absent, or does wink.
Excise men much thy flitting curse,
Since lesser Income swells their purse.
For what thou drank'st, by some is said,
To make ten of 'em thrive o'th' Trade.
In vain *Town-Musick* seeks to cheer
Our griefs, whilst sprightly *Ben's* not here.

For

For without thee the Boy that fings
Is hoarfe, his Fiddle wanteth ftrings,
All that to *Church* on *Sundays* come
Wifh thou wert there, or all elfe dumb ;
Since without thee they howl, not fing :
Like jangling Clowns that cannot ring.
They aim at *Pfalms*, as do the *Chymes*,
And fpoil 'em worfe than *Hopkin's Rhymes*.
When thou wert here all did admire,
To hear both *Organs* and the *Choire*.
Thy *Voice* form'd theirs: when thou didft fing,
Thou wert both finger and the ftring.
Thou mad'ft the Tune ; and all men fay
Thy breath did make their *Pipes* to play.

The P E E K of *Tenariff.* 1660

To my dear Br. Mr. W. Shipman, *Merchant.*

Talk not of *Mount Parnaffus* ! fince I write
Of fuch a fubject as tranfcends its height.
Where th' Mufes cannot mount ; their *winged fteed*
(Tho Fame and Lightning cannot reach his fpeed)
Muft flagge below, when he would try this *Cliff*,
And foar up to the *Pyke* of *Thenariff.*
Some *Hills* are *perruk'd* o're with Trees and Snows,
Others wear wreaths of *Clouds* about their brows ;
But thou, imperial *Mount*, art more renown'd ;
Since thou art only with the Heavens crown'd.
Olympus and the hills of *Arrarat*,
Compar'd to thee, feem as a lowly Flat.

Pelion

Pelion and *Ossa* (though they proudly bear
Their heads) poor *Dwarfs,* yet but as *Footstools* are.
Other great *Mountains* (though not half so high)
Weary the Foot, whilst thou dost tire the Eye:
Thou art * *Sol's Fornace,* where he lights his *Torch*
When he first peeps from out the *Eastern* porch.
Had those old Gyants known thee when th' assail'd
The Gods, their *Palace* they had eas'ly scal'd, *On its
Had *Nimrod* ever of thy tallness known,   Summit is
His *Babel* never had been thought upon.   a hollow
Had *Noah* of this *Mountain* e're heard tell,   fire called
The *Ark* had useless been, and he as well.   *Celdico.*

Was now my Muse as quick of foot as you,
(Who here climb'd high as ever Eagle flew)
She then would trace your steps; and in the Story,
Prove that *high Peek* some leagues below your glory.
Hannibal's march o're th' *Alps* needs no such stir;
Since it was feazible with *Vinegar.*
Sack here was requisite; which Poets sing || A flying
Can mount one higher, than an *Eagles* Wing;   Horse.
|| *Astolfo's Horse* (which *Ariosto* quotes)
Was fed with *Grapes* (no doubt) instead of *Oats,*
That gave him Wings! my *Pegasus* might dare
To mount as high with the same *Provender.*
And since such store does from your *Islands* come;
If you would see him soar, pray send him some.

An

An Hyſtorick Poem. 1660.

Upon the bleſſed Reſtauration of his Sacred Majeſty
Charles the Second, &c.

The P R E F A C E.

THough theſe *Thoughts* gain not *Charls* his ſight,
    To give him his, gives me my right.
And yet now to approach ſo near,
May rather dazzle me, than clear.
Since *Mercury* is ſcarcely known
(Though *Prince* of *Wit*) when near the *Sun.*
Loyalties due, although not heard ;
And, Vertue-like, brings its reward.

From *Mount Parnaſſus*, my deſire
To *Sion* ſometimes does aſpire.
I thought it but a fitting ſtate,
That *Muſes* on the *Graces* wait.
From hence let not the *Reader* fear
I am a *rhyming Presbyter.*
As tho my *Muſe* (when but a Child)
Did go to School to *Robin Wild.*
Or that my *Pegaſus* would ſtoop   *A Rhyme-
To ride in * *Captain Wither's Troop.*   ing *Presby-
    terian.*

But ſtay, amongſt the Rhyming croud   ‖ A Trumpeter
I 'ſpy ſome Wits whom Fame makes proud.   to Rebellion,
* Whoſe *Lawrel-wreaths* on *Cromwell* ſeen   in his *Nec ha-*
(Though he be wither'd) are yet green.   *beo,nec careo,nec*
That Leprous *Syrian* they admit   *curo*; a Book of
To waſh i'th' *Jordan* of their Wit.   his in Rhyme.
     *Vid.*his famous
     Panegyric.

Not

Not for to cure him, but to pleafe;
They made him proud of his *Defeafe.*
Though fome of thefe i'th' *Front* appear;
I'l *Mufter* too, if but i'th' *Rear.*
And though their *Cannons* loudly roar,
Some found comes from my *Piftol-bore.*

The Reftauration and Welcome.   1660.

An Hiftorical Poem upon the Return of King
Charles *the Second.*

GReat *Britain's Soyl,* like *Ægypt's,* fertile turn'd
    By overflowing of its *Natives blood:*
Thus did the *Compoft* of the *Houfes* burn'd
    Fatten the ground where *Priam's City* ftood.

Her Bofom fcarce was more bedew'd with rain,
    Than with thofe precious drops her Children bled;
And manur'd with the heaps of Bodies flain;
    She grew fo rank, that only *Weeds* fhe bred;

Such *Weeds* as fuck'd the *heart-blood* of the Land,
    Smother'd each fruitful Plant and pleafant Flower.
So did the thin bad *Ears* of *Pharoh* ftand ,
    And all the full and hopeful ones devour.

Nor could the *Shrubs* think much at fuch a blow,
    Or know how to divert the fatal ftroak ;   (low,
When thofe curs'd Rebels that brought them fo
    Cut down, alas ! Great *Britains Royal Oak.*

A

A Crime that blasts our former Lawrels won,
    Sullies those Trophies that our Syres did yield :
Saint *Georges bloody Cross* we cannot own,
    Since now 'tis lost within a *bloody Field.*

What hope of future Glory, or of Fame?
    For with the Sun the wasting light must go ;
And we have lost, to our eternal shame,
    Not only *Honour*, but the *Fountain* too.

Success mean time did the bold *Rebels* crown ;
    Success ! too oft the thieves, and Murd'rers boast:
Prosperity brings seldom true renown ;
    Since oft' they merit least, who thrive the most.

If *Wrongs* may be esteem'd by their *Success* ;
    Let us praise *Cæsar*, who inslaved *Rome*,
And think that richer *Crowns* their heads must bless,
    Who caus'd, than those that suffer'd *Martyrdom.*

Worth, when opprest, finds all its Solace here ;
    This quickens *Hope* (that *Shield* against distrust)
Without whose arguments, weak thoughts may fear
    There is no resurrection from the dust.

Faith (that great *Optick*) whose quick piercing force
    Fixes the wand'ring glances of our eyes,
And guides (like *Galilæo's Glass*) their course,
To make *Discoveries* above the Skies ;

By whose clear evidences we possess
    Heaven in reversion, and dispairing scorn ;
By whose *Philosophy* we surely guess
    The Sun, tho set at night, will rise i'th' Morn :
                           'Twas

'Twas this kept us alive ; for hopes that are
    Founded on reason, credit may obtain :
Since to our *Charls* Heav'n did such blessings share,
    We could not think that he was born in vain.

We might as well conclude tho glorious Sun
    Had, to no other end, his light bestow'd ;
Then idly round about the World to run,
    And that his quickning Beams but vainly glow'd.

Altho he from his Kingdoms were exil'd ;
    Forein experience did increase his store :
Thus in afflicting *Job* was *Hell* beguil'd ;
    Since he at last was richer than before.

Nor did it show as Heaven took not his part,
    Because his fortune before theirs did fall ;
Since he who shar'd in the *Almighty*'s heart,
    Was persecuted by a wicked *Saul.*

Most men did fear our happy dayes were done,
    Since *Charls* (our joy) was clouded from our sight;
The *World*'s end thus is guess'd because the † Sun
    Grows lower than it wonted, and less bright.

      † Since *Ptolomy* took its height 1400 years ago, its height is de-
    clin'd 30 minutes.

But thanks to Heav'n we happily mistook,
    And now rejoyce in our deluded Eyes:
The blessing came when we least for't did look :
    The Sun thus lowest seems just at its rise.

Mans

§. 2.

Man's life's a Sea ; when fortunate, it's smooth,
    But when afflicted, then the Waves are rough :
Twixt *Storms* and *Billows* toss'd he scornd 'em both,
    Like a *stout Friggat* that is *Weather proof.*

Afflictions, on right objects well apply'd,
    Bring *Crowns* ; as *showers* make our *Roses* grow:
And like to *Gold* within a *Fornace* try'd,
    His splendor's greater and his vertue too.

Phœbus ecclips'd attracts the greater gaze,
    As tho oblig'd more to his loss of light :
Scorch'd with the fury of the *Dog-star*'s blaze,
    The ground's requited by the dewy Night.

Heroick Charls his crosses then esteem'd
    As his *Refiners, Lees* purge richest *Wines:*
Amidst his troubles he most glorious seem'd :
    Incompast thus with Clouds bright *Phœbus* shines.

Inured to Affliction (Vertue's School)
    For future Empire he was made more fit ,
Our Prince here follow'd his great *Master*'s rule ;
    Upon whose brows *Thorns* before *Gold* did fit.

Nor can it as a banishment be said ;
    He only travel'd to increase his store :
Flowr's so transplanted from their Native bed
    Their beauty, sweetness, goodness is the more.

E.   Fur-

Further that Rivers run they more improve:
  'Tis said that things far fetcht our *Ladies* please,
Nothing but worthless *weeds* do float above,
  We dive for *Pearls* into the deepest *Seas.*

§. 3

England still senseless of that happy state,
  Which by a *Prince* so hopeful she might gain,
O're-aw'd by fear, or overswayd by Fate,
  Like stubborn Atheists, will her crimes maintain.

Scar'd by our Crimes, and blinded by our sins,
  We like those salvage *Indians* appear;
Adore the *Fiend,* insnared by his Gynns,
  And pay him homage out of slavish fear.

Thus have I sometimes certain flowers seen, (Shade:
  Whose leaves were shut to th'Sun, but ope to th'
As more obliged to that killing Skreen,
  Than to those beams, from whence they Being had.

Rebellious Scotland first did ope her Eyes ;
  Scotland ! the source of Treason, and our Woes:
From *Charls* the *Second* she expects a prize
  As great as she in *Charls the First* did lose.

In Selling him the price of blood she had,
  And now she sells to *Second Charls* his *Crown.*
Too wily *Scot* ‖ this bargain is as bad,
  Since now for that he must himself lay down.

‖ By tying him to hard and base Conditions, as to take the Co-
venant.

Too

Too high a price for all the *Crowns* on Earth,
   Though all conftellate in one *Diadem* ;
His Vertues well confider'd, and his Birth,
   They cannot him deferve, though he may them.

But let not here *Pofterity* miftake ;
   Boaft of her *Heroes Scotland* juftly dares ;
Condemn not all the *Twelve* for *Judas* fake,
   Heav'n has its falling, well as fixed ftars.

Amongft which glorious Sparks in his high Spherc,
   Shines great *Montrofs*, the glory of his Age ;
Who brave, did like the *Roman Curtius* dare,
   Perifht his Country's Judgments to affwage.

His pious valour lafting glory got,
   When he alone, to aid his *King* durft come :
Thus *Decius* did himfelf to death devote,
   And battled thoufands to preferve his *Rome*.

Heroic Soul ! until all time be gon,
   His fame fhall largely fpread ; until he come
With his firft *Mafter* to the jufteft Throne ;
   And there receive their *Crowns* of *Martyrdome*.

Though not with fuch Poetic fury fir'd,
   His vaft heroic actions to reherfe ;
Yet with a rhyming guefs I am infpir'd ;
   And *Prophecies* themfelves were fpoke in verfe.

|| He who contriv'd thy death, (although *Argyle* || Fulfill'd
   That bloody Fox) before one year he fee,   truly and
Shall, like to *Haman*, both in fate and guile,   juftly.
   Perifh upon that *Crofs* he rear'd for thee.

E 2
                                      Sce

§. 4.

See now what Vertue in a *King* can doe !
   His great example has made *Scotland* good.
To cure her *Leprosie* she now will go
   To bathe in *Jordans* of her Natives blood.

His goodness and his Royal parts have won
   More than whole *Armies* ever did before ;
All *Scotland* now does to his *standard* run,
   To help his other *Kingdoms* to restore.

To *England* (his choice *Vineyard*) he is gone :
   Where though his faithful Servants murder'd were;
He thought they would not to such madness run,
   Or durst attempt to violate the *Heir.*

But she, besotted with her slavish state,
   This blessed opportunity did shun ;
Stood idly, careless of a better fate,
   And though, in darkness, would not meet the Sun.

Thus did she slight her glory, and her pride,
   And to that *Idol-Cromwel* still incline :
So *Christ* was by the *Gadarenes* deny'd,
   Who valu'd him far lesser than their Sw*i*ne.

Though their vast odds, and usual success,   .*At the Bat-
   Sufficient were to cool a *Cæsar*'s blood   tel of *Worce-*
* So undauntedly he charg'd that all confess *ster.*
   Nothing but *Englands* Sins his *Arms* withstood.

Oh

Oh ! that I had now an heroick Vein,
   His brave heroic Actions to relate:
Although his Army lay about him slain,
   His Vertue yet did triumph o're his Fate.

Horatius thus withstood *Porsenna*'s Host ;
   Such was his valour, such his love to *Rome* ;
And leaping into *Tyber*, well might boast
   To make Retreats so was to overcome.

Through *Troops* of foes he undiscover'd rides,
   Till unto blessed *Boscabel* he got :
To little *Zoar*, with his heavenly Guides,
   From blinded *Sodom* so escaped *Lot.*

To him, as to God's *Israel*, was allow'd
   A sure defence against th' *Ægyptian* spight ;
He march'd behind the *Bulwark* of a cloud,
   A *Blind* to those it was, to these a Light.

Not their proclaim'd Rewards nor curious Spyes,
   Nor *Cromwell*'s luck in *Plots,* this prize could win:
As he had been a second *Paradice,*
   His careful *Guardian* was a *Cherubin.*

Blest *Charles* then to an *Oak* his safety owes;
   The *Royal-Oak*! which now in *Songs* shall live,
Until it reach to Heaven with its boughs ;
   Boughs! that for *Loyalty* shall *Garlands* give.

Let celebrated Wits, with Lawrels crown'd, (brows;
  And wreaths of Bayes, ; boaſt their triumphant
I will eſteem my ſelf far more renown'd
  In being honour'd with theſe *Oaken Boughs.*

The *Genii* of the *Druids* hover'd here,
  Who under *Oaks* did *Britains* glories ſing ;
Which ſince in *Charles* compleated did appear,
  They gladly came now to protect their King.

Thus God for him did Miracles create,
  And *Moſes*-like with ſignal bleſſings grac'd :
To paſs the *Britiſh Seas*, was then a fate   (paſs'd.
  Not leſs, than when he through the *Red-Sea*

§ 5.

Thus he (at once both ours, and Heaven's care)
  For landing-place his *Normandy* did chuſe ;
Whoſe glad Inhabitants, with earneſt prayers,
  Begg'd for that bleſſing 'which we did refuſe.

In *Paris* now receiv'd with jealous eye ;
  Nor can we juſtly tax that *Prince's* fear .
Since in his *Chronicles* He may eſpy
  What buſ'neſs our *fifth Henry* once had there.

Thoſe *Titles* that his Birth, and Merits claim'd,
  More than the *League* with *Oliver* did work ;
And that *French King* might be as little ſham'd
  To ſlight a *Chriſtian Prince*, as court the || *Turk.*
  || Not ſeldome uſed by that Crown.

But

But *Charles*, difdaining a *Difcharge* to hear,
    Left that inconftant Prince with fitting fcorn ;
A bafe indignity ! which *France* may fear,
    And *Frenchmen* rue that are as yet unborn.

Yet, in return for this poor fhort retreat,
    Brave York fights for 'em, that he may requite ;
Whofe Valour did the Crown more furely fet
    Upon that Head ufurps his Brothers right.

By whofe brave Actions, *France* with terrour fees
    What he can do, when he an *Army* brings ;
For if his fortune with his worth agrees,
    Upon his *Sword* depends the fate of Kings.

In *Holland* now great *Charls* keeps his *fmall Court*,
    Where he their native bruitifhnefs converts ;
To whom great Foreign Statifts make refort,
    T'adore, and wonder at his mighty Parts.

Oblige him, *Holland*, with thine utmoft fate,
    His wants do now, as thine did once invite ;
Our blood and treafure did advance thy State ;
    Serve him, and thou wilt fully us requite.

And now the great ‖ *Iberian Monarch* wooes   ‖ King of
    His prefence : *Jofeph* thus his *Keepers* bleft.   *Spain.*
A Treafure ! which, when known well, he will chufe
    Before the precious wonders of his *Eaft.*

Here was he fixt ; and patiently did wait,
    Until the Stars each accident did fit ;
Till Heavens prefixed time had ripen'd fate ;
    That we the fruit of all our Prayers might get.

§. 6.

The *Tempeſt*, which for ſixteen years had rag'd,
   Could not continue long it blew ſo faſt,
As men in mortal Agonies ingag'd,
   Their breathings are moſt violent at laſt.

With loud commands the dreadful *Prince o'th Air*
   Summons his *bluſt'ring miniſters* to blow ;
The trembling *Trees* ſo palſi'd are with tear,
   Their *Leaves* not only fall but *Bodies* too.

And 'tis but fitting State ſuch ways to try ;
   Their Roots diſcloſe the Center where they fell
When bloody *Tyrants*, and *Uſurpers* die,
   All paſſages are ope that lead to *Hell*.

Some *Nat'raliſts*, who deeply'r ſearch than *forms*,
   And into th' hidden *Wombe* of *Cauſes* pry,
Preſume thoſe violent *Autumnal ſtorms*,
   Proclame aloud the *Tyrant* now muſt die.

They ſay that *Fiends* did ply the *Bellowes* ſo,
   And over-heat the *Fornace* ſo beneath ;
The intenſe *Air* broke through, and made ours blow
   And raging flames did make the *Ocean* ſeeth.

But 'tis below the candor of a Muſe
   To ſtrike the dead ; 'tis left to abler pow'rs ;
Nor is ſuch weakneſs proper for the uſe ;
   Alecto's laſhes pierce more deep than ours.

Crom

Cromwel (that *bloody Rebell*) being dead,
  Our hopes, like *Sol* in *Winter*, late did rife ;
Which in few minutes after hides its head,
  Or wears a mask of Clouds before its Eyes.

For lo ! our *Cup* of *wrath* again is fill'd !
  One of his *Sons* the *Tyrant* does fucceed :
Although the old peftiferous *Serpent*'s kill'd,
  We ftill are plagu'd with the invenom'd breed.

What hopes although a gangren'd member be
  Cut off, whilft it does to another fpread ?
Hercules found the *Hydra* would not dye,
  Untill he had cut off the feventh head :

Monck our *Alcides* was, the brave *Saint George* ;
  Who to fet *England* free, the *Dragon* flew ;
Deftin'd by Heaven to that mighty Charge,
  And found their *Mazes*, having got the *Clue*.

Before he proffer'd us his helping hand,
  Thofe *Blood-hounds* which the *Nimrod-Cromwel* bred
Thought to have made their Prey of all the Land,
  And on our very Carkaffes have fed.

Then they that *damn'd old Junto* did recall,
  That murder'd King, and Kingdom too inflav'd ;
Thofe *Calves* of *Bethel*, at whofe feet now fall,
  None but thofe few, who firft the *Idols* made.

Such fudden Changes in fo fhort time fhown,
  Buoy'd up our faith, and made our hopes increafe,
Since *Agues* when they fhift, will foon be gone ;
  And change of pain feems like a kind of eafe.

                                                  Some

Some small efforts were try'd to set us free:
　　As weak *Physicians* on *Recruiters* dare
Bestow their skill ; but when the bold Disease
　　Faces about, they leave off with despair.

No *George* but *Monck* is destin'd for the deed,
　　Whose great experience does to him reveal
When to cut off, to purge, and when to bleed ;
　　And now he sees the Wound is fit to heal.

England his *Patient* is : and like a try'd
　　And carefull *Doctor*, he his skill did show ;
He felt her *Pulse*, and every grievance 'spy'd ;
　　And found no *Remedy*, but *Charls*, would do.

Warwick's great *Nevil Albemarl* out-sounds ;
　　Monck is a *make King* too ! whose glorious fame
Shall flourish whilst the Sun with light abounds,
　　Or golden stars shine in their azure frame.

§. 7.

But stay, my Muse, though in his clouded state
　　Thy Wings unsing'd in his faint beams could play :
Dar'st thou, with *Semele*, incite thy fate,
　　And now in his Meridian glory play ?

With thy weak Pinions thou canst not soar high,
　　This weighty Subject such a burden brings ;
But must, like to the cumber'd *Estrich*, fly ;
　　Whose *Bulk* is furnish'd with unequal Wings.

This

This is to spend above our slender rate ;
    The charge will our abilities outvye:
The *Eccho* tho Heavens *Thunder* can *repeat* ;
    And smallest *Brooks* reflect the spatious Sky.

Since all are joy'd, all should their joys declare :
    Low notes do *Musick*, well as *high* compound ;
An *Oaten Reed* may yield as true a share
    Of Love and Welcom as a *Trumpets* sound.

The *Nightingals* (those *airy Poets*) who
    Make *Helicon* of every *purling spring*,
Their choicest Songs not only will bestow,
    But *feather'd Rhymers* welcome in the Spring,

Tho great Wits rob us, and the Springs have drain'd,
    (*Bethesda* to the poor man was deny'd)
Something of use ev'n may from *Mud* be gain'd,
    As by the *Holland industry* is try'd.

The Heart's not best declar'd by finest words ;
    Silence ev'n sometimes great Rejoycements show;
And humble *Turf,* when kindled well, affords
    As much true heat, as *Chips* of *Cedar* do.

Go forward then, and hope to gain excuse ;
    Rags will be hid in such a multitude:
Heav'n, that bestows on all its fruitful dews,
    Will not refuse the meanest gratitude.

                        Behold !

§. 8.

Behold ! when all our hopes were almoſt fled,
    Heav'n did inlighten us him to invite :
From *Faintings* men ſtart up as from the dead ;
    'Tis darkeſt juſt before the break of light.

Nor does it ſhew as we did quite deſpair,
    Becauſe our ſickly faiths ſuch wav'rings have :
Flames are moſt tremulous, that higheſt are ;
    And we leaſt hope for what we moſt do crave.

After ſuch ſtorms our *Rainbow* now appears,
    That voucher of our ſafety is in ſight ;
And glorious *Charls* to joys converts our fears :
    Phœbus gilds o're the Clouds thus with his light.

He is arrived now to *Scheveling Strand,*
    Which gives juſt cauſe to boaſt her of that bliſs ;
And is the happieſt part of all that Land ;
    Since honour'd his laſt *Foot-ſteps* there to kiſs.

Holland that formerly her *Kings* did hate,
    Is ſo with his heroick vertues ta'n ?
Our hot inquires after him they rate
    Worſe than the *Inquiſition* once from *Spain,*

Had he an equal him their King they'd get ;
    But ſince that quite Impoſſible is known ;
|| *Orange* (his Princely *Nephew*) they will ſet || Another
    In's *Father*'s honours, to confirm their own. Prophecy
                                             fulfill'd.

Where,

Where, with m: e reafon, can their hopes be plac'd,
 Then on a b.anch of that renowned *Tree* ;
Under whofe fpreading boughs, they fafely grac'd,
 From nothing, fprung to this fublimity ?

§. 9.

Great Prince, pleafe to regard your *Britain*'s call ;
 Let *Holland* make you no more ling'ring ftand ;
A little longer ftay will murder all,
 And you be King of a *difpeopled* Land.

Behold your *Neptune*, with his *Trident* there,
 Uncrifps the *Billows*, fmoothing them like *Glafs* ;
And fhews now his Allegiance in his care
 That undifturb'd you on your way may pafs.

The fimp'ring waves their *Viceroy*'s call obey,
 And do for you (the *Ocean*'s *Monarch*) wait ;
With ready Shoulders fee they humbly ftay ;
 And if they fwell,'tis pride for fuch a fraight.

The || *Nafeby* (once a *Dipper*) now begins
 To hate that *Title* with repentant fhame,
And hopes to wafh off her *Orig'nal* Sins,
 Being baptiz'd now into *Charls* his *Name*.

|| A Man of War made and fo called by *Oli-ver*.

As the *Demoniacs* newly *Converts* turn'd,
 Some fignal bleffing did on them attend :
So fhe no fooner with his *Name* adorn'd,
 But the good *Spirit* did expell the *Fiend*.

Great

Great *Britain*, like *Tobias* Bride, poffeft,
    Needs here an *Angel* the fame cure to do ;
Of which no fear, when fhe with him is bleft,
    Since *Charls* her *Husband* is, and *Angel* too.

The *Frigat* now the foamy billows plows,
    Whofe burden is beyond the reach of fear ;
And fteered fafely by our Pray'rs and Vows,
    Does both our *Cæfar*, and his fortunes bear.

But here, my *Mufe*, let's leave him for a while,
    Him, whom the *Sea-Gods* chearfully attend,
And all the *Deities* that guard this Ifle ;   (friend.
    Bleft *Charls*! whom now both God and Man be-

§. 10.

Chufe now a place, where thou mai'ft fit and fee ;
    Where his bleft motion may be fitly'ft fhown :
Let *Dover Pier* then thy *Parnaffus* be,
    And *Britains Straits* thy better *Helicon*.

From Sea-ward now turn thine unwilling eye,
    A little cafting it upon the *Strand* ;
There hafty crouds thou quickly wilt efpy,
    Whofe thronging numbers far exceed the Sand.

Look! how like *Images* they ftand unmov'd ;
    Their greedy eyes to Sea-ward fixed fet :
Thus feem'd the *Statue*, by *Pigmaleon* lov'd,
    When the cold *Marble* firft begun to heat.

To

To th' neighb'ring Coafts whole *Brittany* does flock,
    Clings to the *Cliffs*, her only joy to fee:
Andromeda was chain'd thus to a *Rock*,
    And *Perfeus* haften'd thus to fet her free.

No fayl appears yet to her greedy eyes,
    But fhe tormented is with fharp delayes:
Her large Shores eccho round about with cryes
    That all her *Herrings* are turn'd *Remoraes*;

Thofe living *Anchors*, fcarce twelve inches long,
    That mighty fhips arreft when under fayl:
Thus a fmall *Pibble* being rightly flung,
    Did over great *Golia*'s ftrength prevail.

Britain, that does the pangs of *longing* feel,
    This fluggifh motion of the *Fleet* compares
To that flow Beaft *Pigritia* in *Brafile*,
    That fcarcely crawls a League in feven years.

Nearer their end that nat'ral motions be,
    Philofophers maintain they fwifter go;
This motion, like the bleffing, then we fee
    Cannot be natural, becaufe fo flow.

Would now that || *Swedifh* King were *Pilot* here, || *Eri-*
    Whofe *Cap* could point the *Winds* which way *cus.*
Nor does this Wifh extravagant appear,   (to blow:
    Since * *Edgar* (*Charle*'s great Syre) had *Kings* to row.

     * Five petty Kings rowed his Barge over the *Dee.*

                      The

The pious breathings from the crouded shore
   (A brisk West-wind) keep what they pray for, back:
Thus o'r kind throngings that would breath restore
   To fainting Persons, that intention slack.

The *Proverb's* crost : the *Eastern Winds* are best :
   Since now they waft great *Charles* here to his own:
And vye their blessings with those from the *West,*
   By which the *Locusts* were from *Egypt* blown.

Our *Mariners* need not to *Lapland* send,
   To buy false *Winds,* or charm the boistrous Sea :
Since that great *Pilot* does our *Charls* befriend,
   Whom both the *Ocean,* and the *Winds* obey.

No raging tempest can disturb the Sea,
   Whilst he (our greater *Neptune*) is upon't
Charls easily'r may the *British Ocean* sway,
   Than *Xerxes* try to fetter *Hellespont.*

Methinks the Ship, designed for this fraight,
   Should need no Sayles, nor Rudder her to guide:
But *Dolphins* should out of Allegiance wait,
   Upon whose skally backs the ship might ride.

Thus the tam'd *Argo* that did sail to *Greece,*
   Her willing Oars were seen alone to row :
The *royal Charles* brings home a richer *Fleece,*   * Our Ad-
   And * *Mountague* can more than *Jason* do.   miral,

Not *Indian ships* were ever richer fraught,
   Nor did deserve more welcome to the Port :
Although the treasures of the *East* they brought,
   And had the plunder of the *Moguls Court.*

                        Who

Who can the worth of *Charles, York, Glouc'ster* fay?
   Orprize their Values to a juft degree?
Thofe *Triumvirs* ! fit all the World to fway,
   As equal *Conforts* to the *fatal three.*

As they the *Names,* fo they the *Vertues* bear
   Of *Syre,* and *Grandfires,* Princes all renown'd
For brigheft Stars, each in his proper Sphere;
   And each with *Mercy, Wifdom, Valour,* crown'd.

To all of them thou ow'ft thy feveral Vows.
   But here, my Mufe, thy fcarcity is fhown;
Thy Laurel is fo thinly ftor'd with Boughs,
   Th'art forc'd to twift three Garlands into one.

But if incouragement refrefh the root,
   And fortune take from me her wonted frowns;
My groveling Laurels to the Skies may fhoot,
   And I, inftead of *Garlands,* offer *Crowns.*

§. 11.

Come to thofe *ftraits* from whence he once did go,
   The motion does a bleffed *Circle* frame:
A nobler *Ring* ! his property to fhow,
   Than that wherewith ‖ *Venetians* court the *Dame.*
      ‖ They yearly efpoufe the Sea by cafting in a Ring.

But liften now to that rejoycing noife;
   Thofe piercing fhouts that ev'n to Heav'n advance;
Whofe rattling founds makes *Brittany* rejoyce,
   And ecchos terrour to ingrateful *France.*

If fhouts of Peace can make their *Lillies* pale,
    At fhouts of Battle they will ghaftly fhew ;
And if our *Squibs* and *Crackers* make 'em quail,
    What will the *Thunder* of our *Cannons* do ?

Hark ! hark ! a fhout far louder than the firft !
    Behold ! the fwelling *Top-fail* now appears !
All now (like Clouds of Summer thunder burft)
    Melt into fhowers of their joyful tears.

When on this hand I fee the *Navy* there,
    And *England*'s *Coafts* exalted too on that :
The *Royal Charles* may with the *Ark* compare,
    And *Albion*'s *Cliffs* with thofe of *Arrarat.*

Tofs'd by a *Deluge,* caus'd by our late crimes,
    He fafely now approaches *Albion*'s fhore,
(Like *Noah*) to make happy future times,
    And the deftruction of our World reftore.

Before his landing though, his *Dove*'s fent out ;
    That * *Meffenger* of mercy, and of peace.   *His Act of
Him right Heir to his *Father* who can doubt,   Oblivion.
    Since fo much like him in fuch acts as thefe ?

Grant, mighty Monarch, *Britain*'s humble pray'r !
    Let not thy Clemency prove too unkind ;
But let fome Juftice, with thy Mercy, fhare ;
    Left after ages no diftinction find.

If thine impartial eye vouchfafe to look,
    'Twill find that fome did worfe, tho none did well:
Heaven's felf that on great Sinners pitty took,
    Yet the rebellious *Angels* fent to *Hell.*

                                        Altho

Altho there have whole Seas of blood been spilt,
    And thousands sacrific'd on *Charles* his *Tomb*;
'Tis not enough to expiate the guilt,
    Nor wash away one letter from our doom.

Some of the Tribe of *Corah* still we see,
    Such as 'gainst *Gods anointed* did conspire;
All of 'em, like the common Enemy,
    Are to be scourged hence with sword and fire.

We justly then may hope for better times,
    When those are gone, by whom we were beguil'd:
When *Achan* was condemn'd for his base crimes,
    Success again upon the *Hebrews* smil'd.

Your Mercy (th'only *Balm* our wounds to cure,)
    Should be like that within || *Grand-Cairo* found;
Which *Stories* say will not the *Turks* indure,
    And only prosper in the *Christian*-ground.

             || Related by *G. Sandys*, in his Travels.

§. 12.

And now He's landed; Welcome glorious King !
    'Tis fit we branches of fresh Lawrels spread;
And all our Poets their choice Bays should bring;
    To strew the Paths wherein thy footsteps tread.

Prostrate, my branch, and Muse, I here lay down;
    Where if she chance thy Royal foot to meet,
She may prove *Laureat*, and receive a *Crown*,
    Nobler than those, that *Popes* give with their feet.

On what more glorious Subject can we write.
   Or what Theme can more choice of Fanfie give,
Than his great Name? which brings a sure delight,
   For 'tis by it, we and our Verse must live.

'Tis strange that *Verse* should be to *Charles* obligd;
   When Kings were formerly oblig'd to it;
Because his Merits do all Verse exceed,
   And theirs could not attain to what Verse writ.

His Worth is so apparent, Claim so just,
   His Restoration is rejoyc'd by all:
Thus there was not one *Hebrew* did disgust
   The pleasant *Manna* that from Heav'n did fail.

To *London* now he marches, and is there
   Expected, with such longing hopes and joys,
As men condemn'd their welcome pardons hear,
   Or he feels comfort that despairing lies.

Couragious *York*, wise *Glouc'ster* on each side;
   Valour and Wisdom on our Monarch wait:
He in the fortune of great *Rome* may pride,
   When *Fabius* and *Marcellus* serv'd her State.

Thus on the Body both our Arms attend,
   Which for the common good they're bound to do:
And whilst our *Moses*, and his Arms defend
   His *England*, there's no fear of any Foe.

Black-heath presents it self now to our Eyes,
   Where thronging Troops seem like a moving Wood;
Whose silken Colours whistle out their joys,
   As each its loyal *Motto* would make good.

The

The Horſes neigh as he to them were known:
  Bucephalus thus *Alexander* knew.
By their loud neighing at our riſing Sun,
  They (like the *Perſian Steeds*) their Monarch ſhew.

§. 13.

Bleſt *England*! ſince thou now canſt make it known,
  What, to thine honour, has of thee been ſaid;
How foreign Conqueſt thou ne'r nobly won,
  But when ſome King of thine thy Armies led.

Thus of thy *Cor-de-Lyon* thou may'ſt boaſt,
  Who in one Week did ſawcy *Cyprus* win;
Whoſe Sword and courage(more than the *French* hoſt)
  Dazled the eyes of furious *Saladin.*

Thus thy firſt *Edward* (whoſe fame ſtill muſt live)
  When he to captive *Paleſtine* did go,
His very looks did *Ptolomais* relieve;
  Let any judge then what his Sword did do.

Thus thy third *Edward* fought at *Creſſy*-field;
  Where he beat one King, and two others ſlew;
Thus that young *Mars* (his glorious *Edward*) quell'd
  The furious *French* and haughty *Spaniard* too.

Fifth *Henry* (*Europe*'s wonder and thy pride)
  Fought thus at *Agen-Court*, and conquer'd *France.*
Thus thine eighth *Henry* did his *Enſigns* guide,
  And in *Tournay*, and *Turwin* them advauce.

But

But let none think this a diverſion here :
    To him (the Sea) run all thoſe higher floods,
All their deſerts ally'd to him appear,
    And his th' Elixir of their royal bloods.

§. 14.

But ſtay, my Muſe, to ſhorten now the way,
    Whilſt he to his *Metropolis* does ride;
Here let us celebrate the Month of *May*,
    May! the Spring's glory, and the whole years pride.

I praiſe it not, becauſe the ſwelling Vine
    Shews then its Rubies, or the Roſe-tree buds,
Or Lovers, ſtirr'd by Nature's chief deſign,
    Walk amorous mazes in the pleaſant Woods;

Becauſe the Bloſſoms ſmile, or Black-bird ſings,
    Becauſe the Earth is carpeted with green,
Or that the fairy Nymphs now dance their Rings,
    As Crowns deſign'd for *Flora*, by their Queen :

A far more glorious Cauſe creates my Song,
    Since in this Month great *Charles* ſaw his firſt *Morn*
To which a ſecond bleſſing does belong ;
    Since now for us this ſecond time he's born.

The ſame procedure has eternal bliſs,
    Which the *great Word* to all has ſpoken plain,
For, the *firſt birth* brings no true happineſs,
    Nor comes it, unleſs man be born again.

Nor was't enough, that the reviving *Spring*,
　Or pleasant Flow'rs, his *Ushers* did appear ;
More state was fitting for so great a King,
　Which made Heav'n send that * *shining Harbinger.*

　　* A Star appeard at his Birth

Charles has one Star now more than in his *Wayn* :
　To point our *Saviour* out one did appear ;
Both *Heaven* and *Earth* by his blest Birth did gain ;
　We got a *King*, the *Heav'ns* did get a *Star.*

Blest Prince ! whom Heav'n providing for, did place
　A *Star* : thus *Land-marks* serve the *Port* to show
To Sea-men, toss'd upon tempestuous Seas :
　So this directs him where at last to go.

§. 15.

London is ghess'd now by those Clouds of Smoak,
　Whose thick curl'd Volumes seem to reach the Skies :
Thus Priests of old did for great blessings look,
　When *Altars* smoak'd the most with *Sacrifice.*

It is not Fire, nor Vapours, that compound
　Those Clouds, well nigh in Heav'n already blest :
No they are pray'rs and pious breathings found,
　That rise from *Altars* of each loyal breast.

They're vanisht now : and now the Skies are clear ;
　And other Objects meet our wandring Eyes :
Loud shouts, and *Bells* first having thinn'd the air,
　Temples and *Palaces* begin to rise.

F 4　　　　　　*Paul's*

Paul's firſt (that mighty Fabrick) does appear,
 And to the Skies its lofty top diſplay:
Which (*Babel*-like) our Anceſtors did rear,
 To reach to Heav'n, though in a better way.

What, was its height before by Lightning fir'd ?
 Thoſe active *Meteors* (jealous) did chaſtize
Th' uſurping *Steeple* ; that it thus aſpir'd,
 To mount its daring head in higher Skies.

Firſt Charles deſign'd to reſcue it, and thence
 Its fixed glory never could revolt ;
Since his great Piety would ſurer fence,
 Than any Lawrels, 'gainſt a *Thunder-bolt*:

But our great Crimes, like to the Jewiſh Sins,
 Did both the *Temple*, and our ſelves deſtroy:
Though *Charles* (like *Prince Zerubbabel*) begins
 (Now he's return'd) to recreate our joy.

To him ſhe bows her venerable head ;
 Which (after his) ſhe hopes will be new crown'd
Thus, when the *Patriarchs* had hap'ly ſped,
 To *God* they quickly did an *Altar* found.

The *Tower* (by heroick *Cæſar* built,
 Upon whoſe *Battlements* thoſe *Streamers* play)
Pleads how the Tides have waſht away its guilt,
 Which lately came from the repentant Sea.

The ſtately *Bridge*, oppreſt beneath its weight,
 Yet gladly bears great *Charles*, and all his *Train*;
Under whoſe *Arches*, Tides returning wait ;
 Proud to be ſeen beneath him once again.

          Back.

Backwards the Waves with fmiling Eddies roul,
   'Till they again their *Viceroy Neptune* meet;
Who charges all his Subjects 'twixt each *Pole*,
   To fmooth their Paffes for our *Royal Fleet*.

Go on, my Mufe, thou muft not leave him here;
   Into the *Town* thou muft on him attend :
If thou wilt not the *Citie's* joy declare,
   Henceforth the *Drawers* will not be thy friend.

All hearts together at this inftant meet;
   And all his welcome in one fhout combine;
The Crouds are weav'd together in one Street,
   And all their Eyes are thridded on one line.

The little *Pupil* of the Eye contains
   At once the fpatious object of the Skies;
Yet fuch a Miracle in *Charles* now reigns,
   He's big enough himfelf to fill all Eyes.

The *Walls*, inftead of *Bricks*, of *Heads* are made,
   So clofely joyn'd, and orderly they ftand:
And for more Ornament, it may be faid,
   Each wears a *Turky Carpet* for a *Band*.

With Pray'rs, and loyal Vows the *Town's* made fweet,
   Houfes are *Wall'd* with *Men*, *Roofs* tyl'd with *Boys*;
The *Chanels* wafht with *Wine*; *Streets* pav'd with *feet*;
   And all the *Windows* glazed are with Eyes;

                          Come

§. 16.

Come now fhow fervice, Mufe, as well as love ;
    When both Neceffity and I do call ;
Let thy foil'd Lawrels then a *Beefom* prove,
    And fweep the way before him to *White-hall.*

White-hall ! late foyl'd with dirt, with Thiftles grown;
    As commonly is feen, where *Swine* refort :
But here a Miracle will foon be fhown,
    Hee'l make it both a *Garden* and a *Court.*

For wherefo'ere he fets his Royal Foot,
    Soon will the *Red,* and *White-Rofe* there be fhown ;
Since our great *Charles* is their undoubted *Root* ;
    For him both *York* and *Lancafter* do own.

Though now, my *Mufe,* th' haft brought him to the
    Thou may'ft not enter ; for the *Courtiers* fay (*Port*;
Thy *Poverty* will not befeem a *Court* ;
    Although thy Love and true *Allegiance* may.

Thou canft not then, what there was done, relate ;
    That is impoffible for thee to fhow :
But tho thefe Wifhes cannot gain the Fate
    To come to him, may they to *Heaven* go.

The

The S O U L D I E R. 1660.

To the Illuſtrious and High-born Prince, James
Duke of York, &c.

THE litttle *Spot* I on *Parnaſſus* till,
 Were it, *great Prince,* but fruitful to my will,
The *Lawrels* that my ſlender *Stock* allows,
Each day ſhould yield freſh *Garlands* to thy *Brows.*
And tho laſt Month great *Charles* did juſtly gain
The ſpreading boughes, one branch does ſtill remain,
Which ſhortly will a greater thing be thought,
If fitting Wreaths be to thy Merits brought;
Since all the *Lawrels* that the Earth brings forth,
Will be too ſcanty for thy growing worth.

Thine *Anceſtors,* and *Parents,* all were ſent
By Heav'n to be their Ages ornament;
With all their ſeveral Virtues thou art fill'd;
Roſes, and *Lillies Eſſences* diſtill'd.
Thy *Father's* Soul vyes with thy *Mothers* face;
From her thy *Beauty,* and from him thy *Grace.*
Nor is this all; thou muſt more *Juſtice* have;
Prudent with *James,* and with great *Henry,* brave.
Thy Royal *Fathers Crowns* being from him torn,
Wiſe *Providence* ordain'd thou ſhould'ſt be born.
For ſo, what from him by our Sins were ta'ne,
By thy great *Valour* might be won again.
And tho with bold ſucceſs they ſtorm'd the Walls;
Thou (like *Camillus*) had'ſt expell'd thoſe *Gaules,*
But that kind Heav'n in league with us did ſtand,
Whoſe aid did ſave the labour of thy hand.

Thus

Thus *Hezekiah* might devoutly boaft,
When Angels routed the *Aſſyrian Hoſt.*
Whilſt ſuch ones fought for us ; a doubt might be
Whether they took not one of them for thee.
Such is the lightning of thy piercing Raies ;
And ſuch fair Signs of Conqueſt in thy face ;
So true a heat thy noble Paſſion ſtirr'd,
So ſwift the motion of thy flaming Sword.

Nor was't enough, thy Birth did thee advance,
Valour thy Nature, and Inheritance ;
But thou haſt practis'd War ev'n from thy birth :
Like *Cadmus's Soldiers,* peeping firſt from Earth.
The *Martial Skarf* thy *ſwathing-band* was deem'd,
Bullets thy *Nuts,* and *Drums* thy *Rattles* ſeem'd.
Bellona was thy *Nurſe,* with blood thee fed,
Bright *Steel* thy *Blankets,* and the *Field* thy *Bed.*
Alcides's fp'rit in thy young breaſt did dwell,
Who, in the *Cradle* did the *Serpents* quell.
Young *Princes,* bred up in luxurious *Courts,*
(Like *May-Kings*) are alone defign'd for ſports.
Silk Knots their *Colours* from vain *Women* torn,
Nor ſeek they other *Forts* than theirs to ſtorm.
Vict'ry thine only *Miſtris* was, and there
(If ever) thou wilt turn *Idolater* :
Bold *Scythians* ſo a *Spear* did fix in Ground
And there alone their reverence was found.

Nor did thoſe ſullen times infect thy mind ;
Tho fierce as *Lyons,* yet as *Ladies* kind.
This made th' admiring World both love, and fear :
Thy *Grapes* produc'd both *Wine* and *Vinegar.*

Gentle

Gentle in Peace, in War moſt bravely bold ;
Thy *Springs* in *Winter* hot, in *Summer* cold
Compos'd in tumults, and in troubles gay
Thou, like the *Porpois*, canſt in tempeſts play.

Cromwel ne'r thought his buſ'neſs to be done
Whilſt thou wer't ſafe, tho all Foes elſe were gone :
His reſtleſs jealouſie diſturb'd his mind ;
More dangers yet in thee he fear'd to find.
But when the Fates thee in his || pow'r had brought,
He only then himſelf in ſafety thought. || Taken when
Jeruſalem of reſcue thus deſpair'd,   *Oxford* was-de-
And the grim *Saracens* no longer fear'd,   liver'd and im-
When they with joy the *Auſtrian Leopard* ſaw   priſoned in----
|| To hold our *Cor-de-Lyon* in his paw.
But of thy Chaines he was not long time proud: || Eſcaped
He could not keep this *Thunder* in a *Cloud.*   thence by
   help of----

And now thy ſpreading Fame began t' advance ;
Which he did hear, with terrour, out of *France* ;
That found ſcarce, ſettled, when, behold, again
One louder, when thou fought'ſt for worthy'r *Spayn.*
Honour thine int'reſt was, and ſway'd thy heart
To take the juſter, tho the weaker part.
Thus did brave *Guy* the bloody ſtrife decide,
And help'd the *Lyon* as the weakeſt ſide.
Thy brave *Atchievements* made the *Tyrant* quake,
And at the laſt, his Grave for refuge take.

BEAUTY'S ENEMY. 1660.

Upon the Death of M. Princeſs *of* Orange,
by the Small Pox.

HEnce, hence, vain Fancies *!* 'tis a Sin to be
   A witty praiſer of a Miſery.
Like thoſe hard Wits, who name the *Scars*
Upon her *Face, Ennamel,* and bright *Stars.* (make
They crown their brows with *Cypreſs* boughs, and
Garlands of *Flow'rs,* which they from *Coffins* take.
Then ſhould the *Jews,* thoſe hands have kiſt with joy,
That did their *Temple,* and themſelves deſtroy.
Her Eyes, amidſt her torments, ſparkled beams :
Thus martyr'd Saints ſmil'd in their hotteſt flames.
Nor can the *Parallel* be well deny'd ;
Since 'its too true, ſhe *Beauty's Martyr* dy'd.

Fatal Diſeaſe ! thy Spite too oft is ſent,
Like *Sequeſtrators,* on the Eminent.
Thy Crimes, like thoſe of their damn'd Maſters, ſhow
Like them thou ruin'ſt *England* with a blow.
Great Charles his loſs, and hers were near ally'd ;
In them the *Monarchs* of both *Sexes* dy'd.

Moſt cruel Death ! could not one wound ſuffice ?
Muſt ſhe as many have as Heav'n has Eyes ?
Each Spot upon her Face a *Comet* ſhow'd,
Which did, alas, this fatal ruine bode *!*
So do thoſe *purple ſtreaks,* that often ſtand
Upon *Aurora's Cheeks,* tell' *ſtorms* at hand.
This fatal *Mask,* that thus beclouds her Eyes,
Is no deformity, but a diſguiſe.

'Tis but an *Angel's Veil* she now has on ;
For veil'd they are, when they approach the *Throne.*

THE GENTLEMAN. 1662.

To's honour'd Friend Sir Ger. Clifton,
of Clifton, *K. and B.*

TH' *imbalming* Art that checks the pow'r of *Time,*
   And curbs *Corruption* in its very *Clime* ;
That guards our *Carcasses* against the *Foes*
Which in the trenches of the *Grave* repose ;
With whose repairs our *Cottages* are drest,
Till the return of their Cœlestial *Guest* ;
Yet yields to *Verse* : a drop of *Ink* can guard,
From rav'nous Time, more than a pound of *Nard.*
When *Bodies,* by such means, are most kept safe,
Thy lie i' th' *Tombe,* but live i' th' *Epitaph.*
Yet *Verse* (from whence such benefits accrue)
Has a design, and hopes for more from you :
Thus *Kings* of old, whence streams of *Honour* come,
Receiv'd their *Crowns* fro' th' Common-wealth of *Rome.*
Nor does the *Simile* unfit appear ;
Since a whole *Senate's* congregated here.
For your great *Family* did always use
A *Cæsar,* or a *Cato* to produce.
In this one *House* a noble *croud* appears :
The eighth *Sphear* shines thus with a thousand Stars,
Like *Pliny's* fruitful *Tree,* from whose large root
An intire *Orchard* did together shoot.
|| One dreamt a *Vine* sprung from his *Daughter's* Bed,
Whose lofty branches *Asia* overspread ; || *Cambyses.*
                      Thus

Thus *England's* grac'd, and shelter'd by the *Tree*
Of your illustrious-fruitful-*Progeny.*

The *Chanel* of your Blood's unmixt, and free
From *common Issues* ; like to that fam'd *Sea*
Which proudly sucks into its *Womb* profound,
That *Mess* of *Rivers* which did *Eden* round.
You are a rich *compound,* and *Heralds* view
A troop of *Nobles,* and yet all in you.
Your *Person's* a whole *Presence* ; in each Eye
Ten *Heroes* in their mixt *Elixirs* lie.
You are *Mosaick* work, ta'n in right sense,
Where each piece speaks a several excellence.

THE INVITATION. 1662.

To the worthy Lady Mrs. Margaret Trafford.

IT is a Sin to know where *Vertues* are,
   Goodness, and Beauty, and not make a Pray'r
T' injoy 'em ; since then, *Madam,* all can tell
In you these blessings with rich plenty dwell ;
I should be impious, not to request
To see you, and then after to be blest.
Your *absence* is a Judgment, most men say
But little less than that at th' *latter Day* ;
When we shall want by day the *Sun's* great light,
Nor must injoy the beauteous *Queen of Night.*
Black fate! and yet your absence makes each time
Mourn without light, as guilty of the crime.
'Tis true, these *Planets* may be seen, and are
When you are absent ; but they then appear

Like

Like dying *Tapers*, or (with truer fenſe)
Like things that want their prime *Intelligence* ;
That's you! you gild their *Orbs*, and then refine
Their beams by yours, and teach 'em how to ſhine.
'Tis a religious point now to contend
T' injoy you ; ſince you'r more than any friend.
You are a bleſſing, *Madam*, and a Crown ;
For *Vertue*'s ſo, and ſerves you as her own.
How great's your priviledge ? ſince what the beſt
Of *Saints* did ſtrive for, you find in your breaſt.
Your goodneſs will inſtruct you more at large ;
We are your *Creatures*, *Madam*, and your *charge* ;
You muſt be careful of us, and create,
By your rich preſence, a more happy ſtate.
Haſte then, thou true *Divinity*, and give
Theſe bleſſings, that we may be good, and live.

Right **C H O I C E** at laſt. 1662.
To the ſame.

THE *Soul*, too oft in *Coldneſs* loſt,
Stands need of *Zeal* to thaw that *Froſt*.
Whoſe *Sunſhine* can great Vertues bring,
Bloſſom the *Mind*, and make it *ſpring*.
Fir'd with that ſacred heat, my breaſt
Copies in flames the *Phœnix Neſt*.
The ancient *Bird*, conſum'd with Fire,
Revives into a new deſire :
I'th' *Cynders* thrives the hopeful Birth :
As *Aſhes* help t' improve the *Earth*.

G   *Thoſe*

Those will the fittest *Compost* prove
T' inrich my *Heart*, (that *Soil of love*.)
Cutting the *Suckers* from the root
Will make my *Myrtle* branches shoot.
When *Zeal's* to more than one inclin'd,
It is th' *Idolatry* o'th' *Mind*.
Love *canton'd* out, lessens its store :
As many *Sons* make *Kings* ev'n poor.
But *Fate* does so my *Heart* advance,
To be your *sole Inheritance*.
That *Monarch* of my breast (as due)
No *Heyr apparent* owns but you.
The noble *Romans* thus supply'd
By *Adoption*, what the *Flesh* deny'd.
Observing more returns of worth
From *Choice*, than from uncertain *birth*.
Those easie charms that *Nature* move,
Are but the *Childishness* of *Love*.
The noblest *Triumphs*, and more fame
From *Consuls*, than their *Tyrants* came.
Till *Cæsar's* fate did overcome,
And made one *Trophy* ev'n of *Rome*.
My *Heart*, that *Common-wealth* of *Love*,
Like that of *Rome* in this did prove ;
To present *Rulers* It was true ;
But yearly chang'd again for new.
With *Crouds* of *Deities* well stor'd,
And, as they pleas'd it, them ador'd.
Like *Cæsar's*, your attractive sway
Makes it my interest to obey.
And like dull *Mayors* inslav'd by *Gain*,
I boast the glory of my *Chain*.

Th

POEMS. 83

The LIBERAL LOVER. 1662
To the same.

WHat can my *Mistris* want ? whilst I
Lay some small claim to *Poetry* ?
With *Cleopatra* she shall vie.

My boasting shall not her deceive ;
For *Poets*, *Pope-like*, *Kingdoms* give ;
Nay more, can make the dead to live.

Compar'd with *Poets*, *Kings* are poor ;
Kings have done much, but *Poets* more ;
For they made *Gods* for *Kings* t' adore.

If glitt'ring *Pearls* seem richer prize,
I'l millions give ; for my Supplies
Drop daily from *Aurora*'s Eyes.

Rubies and *Saphires* shall not fail ;
With red, and blue *Clouds* I'l prevail,
To drop 'em down in *shining hail*.

If I once say't, I'l surely do't ;
Planets, instead of *Stars*, shall shoot,
And drop down *Diamonds* at her foot.

Of *Silver*, her I'l never stint ;
The *Moon*'s my *Mine*, and the *Man* in't
Shall be the *Master* of the *Mint*.

If *Guinnies* feem the better change,
Phœbus (my *Patron*) fhall advance ;
For *Gold*'s made only by his *glance.*

For all thefe *Riches* I am poor !
Then why fhould I thus feign a ftore,
When really her felf has more ?

Pearls, Rubies, Saphires, fhe outvies,
And all the *Diamonds* of the *Skies,*
With *Teeth,* with *Lips,* with *Veins,* with *Eyes.*

My idle Fancy makes me fin ;
The *Moon*'s not *current,* 'tis but *Tinn,*
Compar'd to th' *Silver* of her *Skin.*

By thefe great truths I am controul'd ;
My *Guinies* will not value hold ;
She's all one piece of *Angel-Gold.*

DARBY-SHIRE. 1663.

*To Mr. P. K. upon his Prolufion to his
intended Hiftory of that County.*

I'L knock at *Gate* ; Who is it lives here ? Ho !
It is a *Palace* by the *Portico.*
The *Porch* of *Solomon* was thus efteem'd ;
Compar'd with others it a *Temple* feem'd.
'Tis thine *Aurora,* which (as *Poets* fay)
Is *Harbinger* to a more glorious *Day.*
Thy *Lady-Fancy* in her *Bed* ftill lies,
This is the *Ufher* that attends her *rife,*

Her

Her *Face* is beautiful, and makes us wooe
T' enjoy the Bleſſings of the *Body* too.
Thy quick *Invention* may be juſtly gheſt
More than half ready, ſince her *Head* is dreſt.
Thy *Preface*, like a hopeful *Heir,* does ſtand
Rich in Reverſion of the *Father's* Land.
The infant-bud that does ſuch ſweetneſs own,
What may it promiſe when the *Roſe* is blown ?
In this ſmall *Handful* thou haſt clutcht ſuch ſtore,
Methinks thy *Country* ſhould afford no more.
Yet *Darbyſhire* is ſo enrich'd by thee,
It now may vie with fruitful *Theſſaly.*
Potoſi Mines, and Rocks of *Bengalay,*
Thine happy Country are more rich than they.
Its *Leaden Treaſures* (that our *Cannons* hold)
We can exchange for *Argoſies* of Gold.
Pearls, Diamonds, Rubies, and ſuch coſtly fraight,
Our *ſmaller Shot* can purchaſe weight for weight.

Thoſe rare *Coal-Mines* (thy *Book* to us here ſhows)
Far greater Miracles than all diſcloſe:
The *Carbuncle* and *Topaz* are out-ſhone;
Here's *Light* and *Heat* too, treaſur'd in a *ſtone.*
Pliny did ne're of ſuch a Wonder write;
Here you may ſee the *Heat,* and feel the *Light.*

Pactolus, Tagus, and thoſe *Eaſtern ſtreams,*
(Whoſe *Pibbles, Poets* have advanc'd to *Gemms*)
Exceed not thy clear *Trent*; when thou haſt told
Its Stream's like Silver, and its Sand like Gold.
Why doſt not witty *Cotton* then invite,
To do thee and his native River right.

G 3   Such

Such *Trophies* rais'd in great *Augustus*'s days,
Their *Founders* were not only crown'd with *Bays*;
But we may see each Leaf was edg'd with *Gold*,
Mecænas Favours in their *Verse* inroll'd.
Nor were their hopes by *Patrons* only rais'd;
Their merits also were by *Poets* prais'd.
Thus when thou dost thy lofty *Building* reer,   Stately Pa-
Stately, as *Hardwick* or as *Chatsworth* are;   laces of the
Thou'lt see the prouder *Wits* make their resort,   *shire*'s, built
And humbly beg admittance to thy *Court*;   by *Elizab.*
Whilst I am justly proud that I may wait,   *Shrewsbury.*
And stand a *Porter* to attend thy *Gate*.   in *an.* Qu.
  Eliz.

Right marginal note: Stately Palaces of the E. of Devonshire's, built by Elizab. Countess of Shrewsbury. in an. Qu. Eliz.

The CRITICK. 1663.

To Captain W. W. *carping at a* Synelepha
in a Souldier*'s Motto.*

WHat Man is free from *Censure*, when
   It fastens on a *Souldiers* Pen?
The best-arm'd *parts* its force may feel
When *Estritch*-like it bites on *steel*.
A *Critick*'s Bolt's of such weak stuff,
It breaks, or turns again at *Buff*.
He that a Souldier thinks to bind
In *Rules*, must tye his hands behind.
They hate a *Concord*, *Discords* are
The only Rudiments of *War*.
They slight such Rules; and boast their fate
In breaking yours, or *Priscian*'s Pate.
It is then vainer to reherse
To them the Niceties of *Verse*;

When

When they will fwear before your Face
That *Synelepha's* are a Grace;
And how they ferve to trim each line
With knots, and make the *Mufes* fine;
That 'tis a pretty apifh *jarr*,
And imitates the feats of *War*;
One word here runs on th' others point,
Another too has loft a Joynt;
A *Synelepha's* but a *skar*
In *Verfe*, and thofe no Scandals are
With *Souldiers*, where they bring more grace
Than *Moles* to any *Ladies* face.
And if a Verfe fhould prove too fhort
They'l have fome lame Excufes for't;
To want a Foot is no more fault
Than for a *Souldier* 'tis to *hault*.

The CHEAP INVITER. 1663.

To the Right Honourable Patrick *Vifcount* Chaworth, *inviting him to Venifon of his own fending.*

YOur Promife I fufpect not in the leaft;
    And tho the *Scripture* calls Believers bleft;
'Tis wife Civility not to reftrain
From doubling pray'rs for what we would obtain.
When *Court* or *Church Preferments* do beftow,
They are not only begg'd, but paid for too.
Whereas you yours more gen'roufly difpence,
And noble are, all at your own expence.
Thus liberal Princes, when they Vifits give,
Exhauft not by the favour, but relieve.

Be-

Befides the bleffing of his Eye, the Sun,
Makes rich the Earth that Winter had undone;
Yet feeks no more reward for all he brought,
Than fome cold water for his Morning's Draught.
And tho, my Lord, I may too juftly fear
You'l fcarcely find a better Treatment here;
You fhall be welcome, and have Thanks good ftore:
And Heav'n for all it's Bleffings asks no more.

KNIGHTHOOD. 1664.

To my honoured Friend Sir Fran. Leek, *being made Knight and Baronet.*

THis *Title* aim'd for Merit, now the *Stale*
For *Fools*, fince *Honour* is expos'd to *Sale.*
Whofe *Chapmen* for the moft part make it bafe:
As *Cromwel*'s Lords brought *Scarlet* in difgrace.
'Twas *Valour's badge*; but now fome new Knights know,
Nor fee drawn *Sword*, but that which *dubs* 'em fo.
This *Glory* was too bulkey, far too wide
For fuch flim *Heroes* in their upftart Pride.
The mighty *Gyant Honour*, vexing, fhares
His *Trophies* to *Pigwiggin-Souls* like theirs.
Like Boys oppreft, in Arms they idly fit:
Goliah's Sword would only *David* fit.

Nor was there any way left to redeem
It's credit, or create a new efteem,
But by your *Name:* fo that which was thought fit
To honour others, you have honour'd it.

Your

Your conftant Soul ftood firm in wicked times;
Which murder'd Loyalty, and favour'd Crimes.
Caftles and *Armies* fell beneath their hand;
Yet you (more ftrong than either) nobly ftand.
That thund'ring force, which made three Nations bow,
Stirr'd not the *Lawrel* on your *warlike Brow.*
Which did not there, as your Protection, fit;
Inftead of guarding you, you guarded it.
So that which as the *Guard* of *Valour* ftands,
Boafts that it took it's Safety from your hands;
And *Fortune*, that does trample on the World,
Yet trampled on, beneath your feet is hurl'd.

This made you watch'd fo by that jealous Crew;
Yet your Souls noble Motions you purfue.
To keep a ftanding Guard they were oblig'd;
And you did always eat, and fleep befieg'd.
They rated you an *Army*, could withftand
The *Body* eas'ly, when they held the *hand.*
And when their Crimes the Blefling them deny'd
To be of yours, they wifh'd you of their fide.
Thus did you force 'em both to Fear and Love;
As did become the Son of *thund'ring Jove.*
Thus them, without a *Sword*, you *Pris'ners* took;
Who flighted *Cannons*, trembled at your look.
Then he that without *Arms* did *Conq'rour* ftand,
What will he do arm'd now with juft command?

GRIEF.

GRIEF. 1664.

Upon the death of my dear S. Mrs. **P. S.**

FArewel, dear Sifter ! precious Soul, farewel !
  Go to thy fitter place, where thou wilt dwell
With thy Companions, fpotlefs *Virgins* ; where
Thy *Veil* will be as *white* as any there :
Of thine own fpinning too, e're thou went'ft hence;
Made up of *Chaftity*, and *Innocence*.
But now, alas, this fad truth I have learn'd,
None can write *Elegies* that are concern'd.
Objects too near, are never feen fo well
As thofe which at remoter diftance dwell.
Grief, when tis gotten to the higheft pitch,
Damms up our tears, and locks up all our Speech.
Groans then prove you articulate! appear
So courteous, Reader, as to drop a tear.
And fince Grief dulls the Mufes ; pleafe to try
Thy fitter *Genius* for an *Elegy*.
And when th' haft loft as dear a Friend as mine,
I promife here to doe as much for thine.

The GIPSIE. 1664.

Upon Betty Bofwel, *Daughter to* Captain Bofwel,
Leader of the Gipfies, *to vindicate her*.

A Gipfie ! no fuch wonder, fince tis known
  How great *Queen Cleopatra*'s felf was one ;
And that *Mark Antony* (whom old *Rome* faw
One of the three that to the World gave Law)
                    Wander'd

Wander'd abroad, leaving his Native home,
A *Captain* of the *Gipsies* to become.
We may as well that *Empress Learning* flout,
Who first from *Egypt* rang'd the World about.

Because black-hair'd, and of a brownish hew,
Must *Madam Betty* be a *Gypsie* too?
The best complexion sure! and all men know,
That lines of Beauty nought to Colours owe.
What though her Cheeks be tann'd? it may be ghest
The shadow only that her Eye-beams cast.
Talk not what *Silver* drops in *Pearls* are found ;
Black is the Water of a *Diamond.*　　　(bright :
Her eyes (those sparkling Gems) hence shine more
Jewels advance their lustre in the night.
There's none who sees her tho, but would be proud,
Ixion-like, to dally with this *Cloud.*

The *Irish* M A S S A C R E.　1664.

Upon Captain Robert Sutton's *death in* Ireland.

BRave *Sutton* ! *Drums* and *Trumpets* fit thine *Herse*
　　More than the slight solemnity of *Verse.*
The *Muses Heralds* may put up with shame,
They are out-sounded by the *Trump* of *Fame.*
'Tis fitter far that thou great *Mars* shouldst have
Close Mourner, then *Apollo* at thy Grave.
Thy Martial *Steed,* with his courageous *Neigh,*
Jostles my　Pegasus out of his way.
Thy *Sword* has carv'd out such a lasting Story,
My *Pen* adds nothing to thy full-grown glory.

Here

Here lies a *Youth*, had but his Stars been kind,
Or Fortune equal to his Birth, and Mind;
He had brave *Sidney*, and those *Sparks* outgone,
Who did at thirty all that could be done.
But none can limm him right, who have not been
Where they might him before his *Troop* have seen.
How he that day made many *Dons* to fall,
When *English Swords* protected *Portugal.*
Where dying *Valour* he again reviv'd:
Like th' Soul, when to a Body newly 'arriv'd.
The lustre that his *Arms*, and *Actions* show'd,
Like *Lightning*, darted through the *Sulph'ry Cloud.*
His beauty then, with heat of fight improv'd,
Had *Venus* seen, she *Mars* no more had lov'd.
Yet was he not provoking, nor did watch,
Like *Tinder* alwaies ready for a Match
He rather seem'd like to the hardy *Flint*,
Cold until struck, tho *Fire* lye dormant in't;
Or like a *Tempest* that is slow to rise.
But woe to him, that in its way then lies!
This made old gallant *Schomberg* so admire
To find new kindled here his youthful fire;
This made him court him every way to own
What he that day deserv'd, the *Lawrel Crown.*

Blind Love! 'twas thou allur'dst him to neglect
Bellona's Favours to gain thy respect.
Who would believe such *Toyes* should *Sutton* move
To leave crown'd *Victory*, and follow *Love*?
The *Moral* he made good, and, to his cost,
Snatch'd at the *Shadow*, but the *Substance* lost.

III

Ill fare thofe charms ! that made him fhun the light,
For vain *Ideas*, only fit for Night !
Nor can, nor fhall fhe thrive but helplefsbe ;
Falfe to her felf, in being falfe to thee !

Farewel, brave Soul ! the raging *Irifh Seas*
Contain not tears enow for thy deceafe.
That rainy *Region*, though it weep each day,
For thy fad lofs does but due tribute ·pay.
Ingrateful *Ireland* ! thou haft coft us dear,
Committing here a fecond Maffacre.

The C L A I M. 1665.

To my honoured friend Sir Clifford Clifton.
To whom is dedicated the enfuing Poem.

SIR, I prefent you here with nothing new ;
   Since what I write now, all before-time knew.
Your Father's merits were i' th' laft Age known ;
And fhall be, when this and the next is gone.
In fuch *Records* they need not up be laid ,
Tho *Kings*, nay *Gods*, of old, have crav'd that aid.
Tradition will preferve it ; whence may come
More good, and wonder, than from thofe of *Rome.*
Yet ev'ry *Poet* now fhould have a fling :
As ev'ry bungling *Paimer* draws the *King.*
But I prefume fo much of Art to own.
To fay the *Picture's* like, tho faintly drawn.
If it be bigger made, than others drew ;
It is that I grieve more than others do.

And reafon good; fince what I have of Fame,
Is only that which from his *Friendſhip* came.
Since then you heir his Goodneſs well as Lands;
I humbly claim my *Portion* from your hands.

The Old-Engliſh GENTLEMAN. 1665

An Elegiac Poem upon the truly honourable Sir Gervas
Clifton, *of* Clifton, *Knight and Baronet.*

§ 1.

IMagine me one toſs'd on ſhore,
    O'rewhelm'd in tides of Grief before;
Come to my ſelf, I now muſt *him* deplore.

　　Men well nigh drown'd cannot invent
　　One word, whilſt any Water's pent:
So *Grief* is ſilent, untill *Tears* have vent.

　　But now my *Sorrow* is wept dry,
　　And I long ſince did *tilt* each Eye;
Tears from my *Pen* muſt now that want ſupply.

　　Yet if I every tear ſhould tell,
　　They would into an Ocean ſwell;
Theſe are but thoſe that in my *Standiſh* fell.

　　But now theſe *Tides* their Banks muſt break,
　　Left ſtanding too long ſtill they make
The clear-quick Streams of *Helicon* a Lake.

Grief

Grief fhows then beft when frefhly wept :
Rofes lofe fcent, if too much fteept ;
And *Manna* mouldy grows if too long kept.

Silent I was when I did come
T'attend the *Sermon* o're his *Tomb* :
When *Sion* fpeaks, *Parnaffus* fhould be dumb.

Though Poets hence are nobleft crown'd ;
They are, alas! too feldom found
To trace their Meafures out in holy ground.

Yet when in *Anthems*, their defires
Are tun'd to th' key of *Angel-Quires* ;
Such Breathings may augment Cœleftial Fires.

'Tis well if *Paphian Lawrels* may
Prefume to fweep the duft away,
Fell from the *Prophet's* feet that *folemn* day.

Efpecially my fading *Bays* ;
Too often wither'd by the Rays
O'th' *Cyprian Star*, whereon young *Dotards* gaze.

Yet if my *Mufe* can now indite
Any thing, that comes near the right ;
Bleft *Clifton!* 'tis become thy *Profelyte.*

§ 2.

'Tis good to treat of *Subjects* fit :
An *Atheift* once of Heaven writ,
And Heav'n was pleafed to convert his Wit.

But

But what can *Wit* or *Verses* do
To his Advance ? alas ! 'tis true,
They may contract his greatness to our view.

Phœbus needs none but his own Light;
Prospectives make not him more bright,
But only serve to aid our *purblind* Sight.

From *Romes Republick* Crowns did come;
But *Verse* can give a nobler doom;
Yet he crowns *Verse*; as *Cæsar* crowned *Rome.*

Poets shall make his *Name* to bear
Live-Lawrels, and inhabit there:
As *Nightingales* on *Orpheus*'s Sepulchres

Yet they who can themselves retrieve
Fro' th' *Grave,* and Life to others give;
Will gladly court his *Shadow* there to live.

§. 3.

'Tis said, the *Pourtraiture* of Wit
Exceeds the Life, and is then fit,
When 'tis not so like us as we like it.

But such vain Rules we now must shun;
Hyperboles are here out-done,
As much as *Candles* are out-shin'd by th' *Sun.*

A genuine Beauty suits each dress;
Bad faces, to their shame, confess
All Art but paints 'em into Ugliness.

Gr

Great mens Defects are oft fupply'd
By *Verfe*, hence *Crimes* derive their Pride:
Thus *Cæfar*'s *Garlands* did his Baldnefs hide.

But no more blame falls to our fhare,
Than to thofe *Chamber-maids*, whofe care
But wafhes *Faces* that before were fair.

If *Truth* fhould never be expreft
But by thofe who can do it beft ;
She might go naked ftill, or thinly dreft.

At *Coronations* 'twere a thing
Moft ftrange, if only great *Bells* ring;
Or none but *Courtiers* cry'd, *God fave the King*.

From low Stops higheft *Notes* are rais'd ;
By poor mens pray'rs none are difgrac'd :
Cæfar did boaft when in a *Cottage* prais'd.

All Wit is here by Grief out-done ;
And Brains diffolv'd, to Tears do run ;
Yet Tears diftill'd thus may prove *Helicon*.

Let never any Poets more,
The help of other Streams implore ;
Here is fufficient to increafe their ftore.

May they amend what I have done ;
By my Defects their helps are fhown :
Thus *Hones* fet Edges , tho themfelves have none.

§. 4.

Variety of choice is such
  A puzzle, few know how to touch ;
So here too little is, because too much.

  Over-great store distracts a mind ;
    Excess of light may strike one blind ;
Friends make us poor, by being over-kind.

  Lately when *Justice, Learning,* fail'd,
    Honour and *Loylty* were assail'd ;
By him alone those *Vertues* all were bail'd.

  Since dead, let's keep his *Name* alive ;
    That if hereafter *Hell* should strive
To murder *Vertue,* It might hence revive.

  Clifton ! a name too big for Verse ;
    Fit only to describe his *Herse* ;
Pens cannot, *Trumpets* should the *Name* reherse.

  So ancient ! some learn'd men afford
    This observation on record, ---
It's likely to have been the *first-made* word.

  Nor at its rising hath it done
    Like to the far less glorious Sun,
Rise by degrees, its very *Morn* was *Noon.*

  Tho i'th' first age It had that height ;
    I'th' last It does remain so bright,
As (tho revers'd) its *Morning* were at *Night.*

Th

The reafon is, It never fhrouds
Its *beams* with any low-born *Clouds* ;
This *Family* is only *Light* in *crouds.*

Strange ! not to find one low defire !
A noble *Climax* ! ftill climb higher !
The generous flame ne'r out ! right *Veftal* Fire !

Heroes are by fuch *Matches* found :
When heavenly *Dew* falls on right ground,
Rofes and *Lillies* in great ftore abound.

Unequal mixtures courfer are :
Velvets appear more rich and fair
Than glitt'ring *Stuffs* made up of *Silk* and *Hair.*

Thofe *Off-springs* that are old and good,
Lofe luftre, joyn'd with common blood:
The filver ftream run out, nought's left but *Mud.*

Hence 'tis each Age they fall more low ;
Their houfes lefs and leffer Grow :
Like thofe of *Gothland* that are built of *Snow.*

The *Sun* has *Mifts*, the *Moon* her *blots,*
Venus her *Moal,* the *Ermin Spots* ;
Th' *Apoftles Judas* had, and *England Scots.*

This then muft be a wond'rous fight ;
Strange *Day* ! that never knew a *Night* ;
A miracle ! no *Shade* attends this *Light* !

Only some busie *Pates* find one ;
And that because too like the *Sun* ;
For our late *Phœbus* had his *Phaeton.*

His Eldest
Son, a most
hopefulGen-
tlem. tho mi-
serable in his
after Years.

Yet this Remark falls to his share,
His *Morning* did most bright appear ;
Heav'n grant his *Evening* prove but half so fair.

But here's some comfort in the Close ;
He that had much might sometimes lose :
Tho one *Star* fell, yet he had many rose.

'Mongst which his *Phospher* does appear :
Bright Star ! mount now thy *Fathers Carr* ;
And may thy Beams (like his) shine long and far.

See with what twisted Rays he shines !
What *Heroes* may spring from those *Loyns*
Where noble *Clifford*'s blood with *Clifton* joyns ?

*Sir Clifford
Clifton.*

§. 5.

But let us now again adjourn
The *Court* of our *Requests* ; and turn
Our Thoughts once more to the great *Father*'s Urn.

An *Urn* ! which precious stuff does line ;
Whose Lustre does quite thorough shine ;
And hereby shews the *Relicks* are divine.

Could *Rome* but of him (as hers) vaunt,
I'th' *Kalendar* she would him paint,
And turn'd *Saint* already to a *Saint.*

But he does no such *Varnish* need ;
Himself did his true Glory breed,
And on its proper Substances can feed.

Cato the period was, and Pride
Of ancient *Rome*; nor is't deny'd
But that Old *England* too with *Clifton* dy'd.

The *Hospitality* of old
(Which gave that Age the name of *Gold*)
He did revive, and afterwards uphold.

The noble *Pyles* those times did rear,
Inviting *Land-marks* did appear,
And gave free Welcome to each *Passenger*.

Not like those, which our *poor-men* call
(And justly too) *Mock-beggar-Hall*;
Where *Rats* and *Mice* do into Famine fall.

Their *Prospects* yield a false delight:
Thus *Nauplius*, with deceitful Light,
The *Grecians* did to barren Rocks invite.

But *Clifton* gain'd no such Report;
By th' entertainment and resort,
It ought in Justice to be call'd a *Court*.

Nor did his vast *Revenues* rise
From *Rackings*, worst of *Tyrannies*;
His *Farms* were *Portions*, and his *Rents* a *Prize*.

He would not such hard *Penn'worths* let,
Like th' *Tyrant Russe*, who in a Pet
Took *Tribute* from his Subjects Rest and Sweat.

H 3   His

His *Charity* aim'd high, and true;
Not like some *Great ones* in our view;
He made as many, as they did undo.

To that proud *Zeal* he ne're did fall,
Alms Houses build in fight of all;
For every *poor man* was his *Hospital.*

Tho still his *Charity* aim'd high'r:
Like *Moses bush,* that sacred Fire
Did not confume it felf, nor yet expire.

All's *Neighbours* he did love fo well;
Although a *Cedar,* Truth must tell,
His drops ne're hurt the *Shrubs* on which they fell.

Amongst thofe *Days,* whofe nipping pow'r
Did almoft blaft each hopeful Flow'r,
And verdant Tree, his *Laurels* fcorn'd to lour.

Bafe Actions he did fo defie,   Having loft
He loft what would an *Earldom* buy,   in the late
Rather than fell one Drachm of *Loyalty.*   Wars 80
thoufand *l.*
at leaft.

Let *Fortune* all her Ills invent;
Like true *Elixir,* his Intent
Improvement did receive from each Event.

Diamonds by darknefs fhew their light;
Oppref's'd like *Laurels,* he's more ftraight;
A *well-built-Arch* is ftronger by its weight.

Tho

Tho *Vapours* clouded *Britains* Sky,
He, like *Pythagoras*'s *Bird*, did fly
Above thofe *Clouds*, and all their Storms defie.

For all thefe *Clouds* he fcorn'd to yield ;
But ftill remain'd like his *rich Shield* ;
A *Lyon argent*, in a *Sable Field*.

§ 6.

After *Great Brittany* had mourn'd
Twelve years, her Sorrows were adjourn'd ;
Her Joys again with glorious *Charles* return'd.

When *Clifton* did attend his *Train*,
How he rejoyc'd, to find again
The ancient Glories of his *Grandfire's* Reign?

Thus *Neftor*'s Blifs he did enjoy ;
In peace his laft days to employ,
After the tedious bloody Wars of *Troy*.

§ 7.

But ftill his *Warfare* is not done ;
There's one Fight more he cannot fhun ;
None truly crown'd untill that *Battle*'s won.

This was, alas! his fharpeft fight;   He died of the
His Pains were a deplored fight ;   Torments of
But moft to us, plac'd in the worfer light.   the Stone.

Th' *Egyptians* only Darknefs 'fpy'd
I'th' *Cloud,* that was the *Hebrews* guide;
'Twas fo to them, Light on the other fide.

Immunity's to none allow'd :
Iris, in her gay Colours proud,
Is made betwixt the *Rain-bow* and a *Cloud.*

in's laft *Mile* he was forc'd to ftay
Turmoil'd with pains: and *Church-men* fay
The Road to *Paradife* is rugged way.

Foes crown us who are hardly bet;
And *Dangers* nobleft Conquefts get:
For *Laurels* flourifh moft when fteep'd in *Sweat.*

Clouds could not fmother all his Beams;
Moft patient in his fad Extreams:
The martyr'd Saints thus fmil'd amidft their flames.

He praying paid the Debt he ow'd;
His laft Breath, whence he had it, fhow'd;
His *Afhes,* like to thofe of *Incenfe,* glow'd.

And now, poor Mufe, clofe up thofe Eyes
Whence all thy Light and Hopes did rife:
The *Sap* being ta'n away, thy *Laurel* dies.

The POET on Foot. 1665. *To Mr. S.*

THO late, I come at laft, this ftay of mine
Carries no more of Rudenefs than Defign;

F

For well I know the common Cuftom's fuch,
That look'd-for Guefts find always chear too much.
Which my weak Stomack never could digeft;
Since too much Expectation daunts a Gueft.
But this, Sir, was not all my *Mufe* kept home,
Conftrain'd by fate, elfe fhe had fooner come.
She wants a *Steed* ; and fhe has got the pride
Of wanton *Girls*, that would on *Cock-horfe* ride:
But the ftrange-*Horfe-difeafe*, that rag'd with us,
Amongft fome others, caught my *Pegafus*.
But tho he did efcape ; He yet does lack
The only *Medicine*, a *Drench* of *Sack* :
Which is fuch coftly feeding this hard year,
Our *Hacknies* will be, than our felves, more bare ;
I mean us *Poets* : For thofe who are able
Keep their *Jades* lean i' th' *Study*, fat i' th' *Stable*.
I loyter'd thus hoping at *Lenton-fair*,
Amongft our *Gallants*, I might borrow there.
Alas, in vain ! unlefs I would fhift thus,
Making a *Hobby-Horfe* my *Pegafus*.

The PICK-POCKET. 1655.

To my good friend Mr. R. Mafon. *raptim.*

IF Clients wants, or follies grant thee paufe ;
Or Sack, which is more powerful than Laws ;
Pleafe to unbend a while ; lay *Ploidon* down,
And *Cook*, the two worft pick-pockets i' th' Town.
They rob with priveledge, and pow'rful hands ;
When the poor Cutpurfe clofe, and trembling ftands.

And

And yet their malice is at them difpleas'd :
Thus *Alexander* a lefs Pirat feiz'd.
The Law attaches Felons when it pleafes :
The Plague fo routs the Pox, and fmall difeafes.
Yet we muft feek its help ; for 'tis well known,
Moll Cut-purfe fought to help folks to their own.
Leave then this Scandal, and repair to me ;
Who, tho half drunk, thirft for thy Company.
Here's Sack, if *Noy* (the quickeft of your Tribe
Had fupp'd, he would have ta'n before a bribe.
Such as will make thee eloquent as *Finch* ;
And yet not eek thy Rhet'rick with a Clinch.
Each drop of which a Ruby will create,
Inriching Nofes at the *Indian* rate.
Hafte then, or we fhall be fo rich and great,
We fhall difdain, what now we do intreat.

The MISTAKE. 1665.

Upon drinking a Glafs of Beer to C. J. B.
for one of Sack. raptim.

PArdon, great *Bacchus*, I repent !
   The Error has its punifhment :
Poor Travellers are cheated fo,
That come where *Sodom* Apples grow.
This change of mine has his difgrace,
Who did, for *Juno*, Clouds imbrace.
Nor is the diftance leffer here ;
Immortal Sack, and Mortal Beer !
So did the crazed *Hebrew* fail,
Deferting God, to go to *Baal.*

Y

Your *Spanish Donna* has a touch
More charming than the thick-skin'd *Dutch*.
One thus a Beauty thought to wed,
But got a *Gypsie* to his Bed:
Beer has that tann'd and yellow hew,
Like hers that did the Liquor brew.
When Sack's Complexion is refin'd;
As though it were with Sun-beams lin'd.

The DISGUISE. 1665.

Upon Mr. Ger. Lee, imputing a scandalous Paper to me, and subscribing his Name covertly within a Circle of inverted Letters.

RAther than suffer this, my injur'd Muse!
  Mount now, and spur thy sku-bald *Pegasus*;
And turn Apparitor. Here's bastard Wit
Laid at thy Door, if thou wilt Father it.
Observe the Castling well! What, no Wall-eye,
Mare-face, or Mark, to know the Stallion by?
Look there at lowest end a Buttock-brand;
A Transcript from that in the Father's hand.
His shrivel'd Name (fit for a larger Stage)
Shows like to *Bajazet* within his Cage;
His envious-black-mouth'd Verses make it said
A Knot of Snakes, torn from *Erinnis* head.
A peevish Fiend within a Circle shut;
Homer's fond Fables ramm'd into a Nut;
A Knave in Fetters; *Gotham* in a Map;
A crafty Fox caught justly in a Trap.

Thy

Thy Name, methinks, peeps forth, and seems to be
(As th' Owner ought) upon a Pillory.
Justice triumphant is ; nor can it choose,
When such a Hang-man's catch'd in his own Noose.

The MERCHANT. 1655.

Upon the Death of my Br. Mr. S.S. *in the* Canaries.

WHO knows his Fate, or where he shall expire,
'Tis comfort tho, that Heav'n is no where nigh'r
Than where we dye. The Grave's an humble rise,
From whence we take our leap into the Skies.
A true Enlargement Death for all prepares ;
Takes cares from Young-men, and Old-men from cares
Let us not then his loss of hopes deplore ;
Those who have full Injoyments, hope no more.
Hope is the Balm of Life, and Balm is found
In vain, when we no more can have a Wound.
Nor could long Life have much advanc'd his Story,
They have gain'd full enough who have gain'd Glory
His vertuous Inclinations claim that State ;
Such early hopes attract the smiles of Fate,
Nor did he vainly suck in foreign Air,
Since half the World now claims in him a share.
A Life to him his loved *Europe* gave ;
And *Africk* did bestow on him a Grave.
Those Isles to him did fortunate appear ;
And he gain'd well who purchas'd Heaven there.

The CAVALEER. 1665.

An Elegy upon Capt. Ben Marſhal's *Death.*

O'Rwhelm'd in *Night,* and *Grief* I ſit ;
 For *Verſe,* or *Humour* moſt unfit :
Aurora's Mother both of *Joy,* and *Wit.*

By day, the *Chanters* of the Spring
 Warble, and keep time with the Wing ;
But yet by Night the *Nightingale* does ſing.

'Tis *midnight* now, and all at reſt ;
 Except the *ſorrows* in my breſt ;
Which are ſo far from ſleep, they yet are dreſt.

For Verſe is Grief's moſt-Solemn dreſs ;
 Verſe, more than tears, can grief expreſs ;
Such 'drops their laſting fountains muſt confeſs.

For tears (tho from a double *Rill*)
 Are ſometimes dry, the Brain ſprings ſtill ;
It is the *Conduit,* and its *Pipe* the *Quill.*

Let none ſay Verſe may leſſen **Grief** :
 David (altho the *Poet's Cheif*)
His tears fro' th' Muſes fountain got relief.

No artifice is needful here
 (Like *Herod's*) to exact a tear ;
His loſs its ſelf's a general Maſſacre .

Who order'd all his Nobles after his Death to be murder'd ſo that it might be attended with general ſorrow

He

He such true Friendship did possess,
As might its wasting stock increase,
And furnish this our jarring World with Peace.

Such a *Companion* all would crave,
Or such to be, or such to have;
Nay we for him did *Wine, Plays, Women,* wave.

To prove his *Inclinations* right;   He went to assist
His *Loyalty* was his delight;   the King about
For tho a *Boy,* he left his Play to fight. sixteen Years
                                    old.

Those *Wounds,* which for the *King* he met,
Spoke glorious Toils; for *Blood*'s the *Sweat*
Of *Honour,* the best *Scarlet* Souldiers get.

Tho Fortune (to maintain her spite)
Did aid the Wrong against the Right;
He courage shew'd in Suffrings, as in Fight.

In *Persecution* he had share;
Yet Patience did that smart repair:
So *Thunder* troubles, and yet clears the *Air.*

As in those days he scorn'd to bow
To any *Tyrants* threatning Brow;
So he disdain'd as base a crouching now.

For though his Worth could not be heard
He knew it was it's own reward;
Since Traitors were prefer'd, he favours fear'd.

It would but our devotion blame,
Alone the inward *Rites* to name,
And quite neglect the stately *Temples* frame.

Such was his *Body*, strait and high;
And then the Chrystals of each Eye
Did well reflect the beauties of his *Sky*.

His *Body*'s strength, like to his *Mind*;
That we despair in one to find
Their equal, 'till at last again they're joyn'd.

Fruits ripest sooner suffer wrong;
This made him dye, alas, too young:
'Tis hard to run so fast, and travel long.

That *Conq'rour Death* (to name him right)
Durst not trust here to his own might;
But cowardly avoided open Fight.

H' attackt him like a wily Foe;
Wasted his strength without a blow;
And kept aloof till sure to find it so.

Yet still mistrustful to prevail,
With all his force did him assail;
Yet till the last his *Heart* did never fail.

Thus Martial *Troy* (that *Gods* did build)
Defended by the sacred *Shield*;
When all was lost, the *Temple* then did yield.

His

His EPITAPH.

TRue *Fame*, from *Envy*, takes no wrong;
    Where Merit is. *Stones* find a *Tongue*.
And this declares --- Here lies inclos'd'
A *Body*, was so well compos'd
For strength, and beauty ; none could find
An equal to it, but his *Mind*.
Heav'n has his *Soul*, the World his *Fame*;
We only can his *Body* claim.
Death (that great *Chymist*) has refin'd
The *Oare*, and left the *Dross* behind.

The GOSSIPS. 1666.

To Sir Clifford Clifton, *for a Buck against
a Chrift'ning.*

MY fate is, when I write to you,
    To own old favours, or beg new.
Not strange with *Poets* ; since an *Alms*
And *Thanks*, make up the Book of *Psalms*.
'Tis lawful, when, like th' *Alms-house* wont,
The *Benefactor's* shewn i'th *Front*.
My *wants* need no more *Vouchers* take
Then that I *Verse*, and *Children* make.
Both got in an odd itching Vein ;
Expensive to the *Purse*, and *Brain*.
Yet of the two *Children* are most ;
With labour born, brought up with cost.
Especially since *Gossips* now
Eat more at *Christnings*, than bestow.

Forme

Formerly when they us'd to troul
Gilt *Bowls* of *Sack,* they gave the *Bowl*;
Two *Spoons* at least; an use ill kept;
'Tis well now if our own be left.

Since Friends are scarce, and Neighbours many,
Who will lend mouths, but not a penny;
I must (since poor, as almost may be)
Thyestes like, cook up a *Baby*
Or if you grant not a supply,
Must ev'n provide a *Crisome Py,*
It will be tenderer then Gelly,
So long parboil'd in *Mothers* Belly.

Venus and *Mars* Conspirers be,
And frown'd on my *Nativity.*
My Fortunes, first by *War* o'rpow'rd,
And now, alas, by Love devour'd.
Children will rob what *Round-heads* left;
Yet we make blessings of the theft.
The gain's soon told, if we compare
Our joy with grief, our hope with care.
Children grow up as we decay,
Their structures on our Graves they lay
And *Christning-Feasts* are but a *Toll*
Exacted, or an earlier *Dole.*
A *Font* brings far the heavier doom
To a poor *Father,* than a *Tombe.*
We're brought to th' *Grave* with Solemn state,
Where *Friends* and *Mourners* kindly wait:
Worms on our *Corpses* only thrive;
But *Guests* devour us here alive.

I

To you the Pow'r, Sir, only falls
To save me from these *Canibals.*
A *Buck,* you know, oft' stops the fury
Both of an hungry *Judge* and *Jury.*
Please to bestow one ; He shall run
In four *Parks* then, instead of one.
Wee'l follow th' *Chase* so, that he shall
Be forc'd to leave the *Crusted Wall*;
'Till to the inmost *Copse* he skips,
Pal'd round with *Teeth,* and *hedg'd* with *Lips.*
There *Blown,* and *hot* we will design,
To make him plunge in *Ponds* of *Wine.*
Then, Sir, your *health* begun shall be,
As *Crown* to the *Solemnity.*
And he who dares that *health* disown,
Shall have the *Horns,* and not the *Crown.*

The PARTHIAN ARCHER. 1666.

Upon a Spanish Needle run into a Ladies Breech.

WELL hit, small *Don* ! I'le now protest
　　That *one-ey'd Marks-men* aim the best.
Thy piercing Charge none can withstand,
When guided by a *Ladie's* hand.
S'attractive, and so fair a *Mark,*
A man might hit, tho in the dark.
Such a white pair of *Butts* ev'n wo'd
Make all men shoot, like *Robin Hood* ;
Whose steady aim such credit got,
It never mist to cleave the *Mott.*
All would with *David's Slingers* dare,
And aim their *stones* to hit the *Hair.*

Sha

Sharp *Spanish Pike* ! that can prevail
To wound her through the double *Mail*
Of *Coats* and *Smock* ! when *Cupid*'s *Cannon*
(Mounted on wheels that it does ftand on)
Thunders in vain on that defign,
And's forc'd at laft to undermine.

Sure *Cupid*, thirfting for fuch drink,
Approach'd fo near the *Fountain*'s brink ;
And pierc'd that *Butt* whence he did know
Rich *Nectar*, tunn'd up there, would flow.
The waving *Needle* here does fix,
And fteady againft her *North-ftar* fticks.
Hence that *Magnetick* power does come ;
No *Loadftone* to a *Lady*'s *Bumm*.

The CANARY ISLANDS. 1666.

To my dearly beloved Brother,
Mr. William Shipman, *Merchant there.*

COme *Bacchus*; God of *Poetry*, by right ;
Lend me thine influence, whilft now I write.
Thy *Sackbut* can into my breaft infpire
More active heat, than can *Apollo*'s *Lire.*
He's an *Ufurper* ; and his pow'r a crack,
If we his *Helicon* compare with *Sack.*
Lock up that *Nectar* but a year or two,
And fee what all his *Hippocrene* can do.
That *Trough* of *Pegafus* ! a pretious grace
To vaunt thus of an *Hackney*'s *wat'ring*-place !

Not the leaft fpark of Wit it can infpire,
Without affiftance both of *Malt* and *Fire.*
When *Heat* within the lufty *Grape* does grow,
'Tis to it's felf *Malt, Heat,* and *Water* too.
A Pipe of *Sack* (which is great *Bacchus*'s *Throne*)
Is both *Parnaffus* and a *Helicon.*
Juno her felf and *Venus* too are dull,
If *Hebe* do not fill their Glaffes full.
New Vigour to their Eyes it does afford ;
Mars fwears it whets his *Courage* and his *Sword.*
The Spirits of *Jove* himfelf are dull as Lead,
Without this *Nectar* fill'd by *Ganimede* ;
He's one of *Bacchus*'s Drawers. *Sack* creates
Life in thofe *Gods* that do direct our Fates.
See the Injuftice then of lying *Fame!*
Bacchus deferves, *Apollo* gets the Name!
Thus *Princes* in their *Wars* fill up the *Story,*
When their brave *Generals* deferve the Glory.

Bleft Soil! that does diftill fo rare a *Juyce,*
More precious far than *Canaan* did produce.
The *Milk* and *Honey* which did thence proceed,
Made only naufeous *Butter-milk* and *Mead.*
Whofe Influence more of *Phlegm* than *Blood* did breed
Difperfing Weaknefs through the *Jewifh* Seed.
Made them defift and give their conqueft o re,
Truckling to thofe they trampled on before:
When as the haughty *Spaniard* did decline
Tho Univerfal *Monarchy,* 'till *Wine*
Infus d that lofty Spirit in his Veins;
And more by that then by his *Sword* he reigns.

Bd

Bold *Britain* does her *Trophies* here decline,
As never conquer'd but by *Spanish Wine*.
Their mighty *Navy*, tho she forc'd to wrack,
Yet falls beneath the *Puissance* of *Sack*.
Had *Sack* been the Commodity, the *Day*
Had lucky been at || *Rheez*, as *Tercera*. (known
French-Wines work small efforts; as may be
By th' Spirits, which in *Gallick* veins are shown.
Their *Wines* and *Spirits* both alike are vain ;
Soon kindled, and as soon piss'd out again.

We were worsted at Rheez by France, but came most gloriously off at Tercera against Spain.

Wonder then, that we fall not out with *Spain*
On purpose, those rich *Islands* to obtain!
Our *English youth* would all its valour try,
In one six months to win, and drink 'em dry.
Wee'd rigg out such a *Fleet* that all the Ground
Should scarce sufficient be for *Ballast* found :
And that high *Peek* there should the honour gain,
To be *Main-mast* i' th' *Royal Sovereign*.
The *Rhyming Tribe* would rally all its store,
And strive to charm the *Dolphins* to the Shore,
Where on their scaly *Saddles* they might sit,
Serving as *Trumpets* to th' *Canary* Fleet.
Whose ecchoing blasts, like those of Flame, would do;
Incite their courages, and crown 'em too.
What rich Incouragements might hence needs flow ;
When they at once *Lawrels*, and *Life* bestow ?
Their share should then be double, as their pains ;
Because their private, would be publick gains.
For *Sack* is only proper for the use
Of *Poets*, who can best preserve the juyce.

Which

Which when diftill'd by active heats o' th' brain,
Is all th' *Elixir* that our *Chimifts* mean.
Churchmen and *Poets* might increafe their light ;
Since *Pfalms* and *Plays*, both may be better'd by 't.
None that could get a *Boat* would ftay behind ;
Our very breaths would ferve us for a Wind.
Nay rather than be abfent on this Quarrel,
There's fome would venture over in a *Barrel* ;
Defpifing Tempefts, and the fears of *Wrack*,
With very hopes of filling it with *Sack*.
Cowards would gladly bleed a *Quart* in fight,
To drink a *Quart* of dearer *Sack* at night.
And this does prove *Bacchus* the God of *War* ;
Since he alone can make a *Dutch-man* dare.

If you would kill thefe *Boars*, let 'em not root
Within a *Vineyard*, and you'l furely do't.
Keep 'em from *Brandy*, and from other Wine,
Thefe *Holland Boars* are worfe than other Swine.
O, for fome Devillifh *Swine-herd*, to convey
This Herd, like th' *Gadarenes*, into the Sea!
But this conclufion is not lately found ;
Like th' *Devil's Darlings*, they will not be drown'd:
Except by one attempt, which cannot fail ;
When we get *Sack*, let's lend 'em all our *Ale*.
Which foon its wonderful Effects will fhew,
And drown them, which the *Ocean* cannot do.
Hail, mighty *Bacchus* ! thou haft won the Field ;
Mars and *Apollo* both are forc'd to yield.
Claim then the *Empire* due to thy deferts ;
And henceforth reign thou *God* of *Arms* and *Arts.*

The

The Old MOURNER. 1667. *To Sir* J.D.
Upon an Old Mourning Suit.

WHAT am I like now? do not fpare :
  A *Vicar* preach'd thred-bare ;
Or younger Brother left to th' *Heir.*

Worth waits not alwayes upon ftore ;
  Defpife not then the poor ;
Mock not a *Cripple* for his Sore.

Silk cannot make each Wearer fine ;
  Nor does Gold only fhine :
Tiffue wears out, unlefs you line.

I flourifh't once (I fpeak aloud)
  As you, be ne'r fo proud :
Phœbus himfelf may meet a Cloud.

Will *Mourning,* think you, frefh appear
  After 'tis worn a year ?
You may as well expect a tear.

Yet I could mourn fix twelve months more,
  Upon a Lawful Score ;
And I have *Friends,* I hope, in ftore.

My *Black-Coat* fpeckt you call white *Ink* ;
  Or tears o' th' *Tankard* think ;
Why *Grief* is thirfty, and muft drink.

Grief's a *Good-fellow,* as appears ;
  For he will *tipple* tears ;
Your thirfty *Mourner* merits Jeers,

    I 4   True

True Grief will make one lean appear ;
    Conceit each thrid that's bare
A *Rib*, by Grief confum'd fo near.

Each mournful *Hole* that you efpy
    Imagine then an *Eye*
Wept out, and that's more than *wept dry*.

My peeping *Shirt*, through every Chink,
    Perfwades me much 'to think
I'm like this *Paper*, blurr'd with *Ink*,

GRATITUDE. 1667.

*Some grateful Acknowledgments to that moſt ex-
cellent Poet,* Mr. A. C.

HEnceforth, my *Muſe*, more boldly claim the *Bays*,
    Ennobled now by *Cowley's* generous Praiſe.
Apollo here has filver'd o're thy ſhades:
Thus *Lords* can *Ladies* make of *Chamber-maids*.
Thou art a *royal Miſs*, and now muſt get
No leſſer Honour than a *Coronet*.
Nay, richer Bleſſings *Cowley's* Praiſes ſhare ;
Now thou'lt be thought both vertuous and fair.
Such plenteous Contributions to the Poor,
Proclaim his Soul as large as is his ſtore.
The Sun is no leſs glorious in his Blaze,
Although he gild the lower World with Rays.
His Beams thou muſt reflect, and grateful prove,
And nouriſh in thy Breaſt his kindling Love.
'Twill bring effects worthy his virtual Powers,
Making thee pregnant both in Fruits and **Flowers.**
                     Fd

For that which bloſſoms not with *Cowley's* Praiſe,
Is but a ſapleſs branch of wither'd *Bays*,
Warm'd vainly by *Apollo's* quickning Rays.
Without his Light, vain are the quickeſt Eyes;
His influence, ev'n from *Duſt*, makes *Inſects* riſe.
Such mighty Sums 'tis eaſi'r to repay
When they're not lent, but freely giv'n away.
Like heav'nly Bleſſings upon thee beſtow'd,
To make thee thankful and thy Works more good.

Hail *God of Wit! England's Apollo*, hail!
Thou art no Off-ſpring of an *idle Tale*,
Like *Homer's Deity*. But ſince that ſame
All Ages gave him, is thy proper claim;
Accept the Veneration and the *Name*.
Fulfill'd in thee is what the *Ancients* feign,
And *Pallas* is the *iſſue* of thy *Brain*,
As th' *Muſes* of thy *Wit*: when ſafely laid,
Of thy *firſt-ſheets* their *ſwathing Cloaths* were made.
Others there are would thy fair *Off-ſpring* claim;
Theirs (by their want of heed) o're-laid or lame.
But when it comes to Tryal they reſign;
Juſtice decrees the *Living Child* for thine.

The *Muſe's Empire* bears ſo great a Name,
Thou haſt two *Rivals* in thy *Lady-Fame*;
Waller and *Donne*. You are the only three
Who juſtly can pretend that *Monarchy*.
Donne's Judgment, Fancy, Humour, and his Wit,
Strong, ſearching, happy, and before ne're hit,
Gives him a fair pretence to climb the Throne;
But *Waller* rather ſtops than plucks him down.

Rich

Rich he appears; his courtly Vesture grac'd
With golden *Similes* all over lac'd.
But *Cowley* (like the *Infant* of the *Sun*)
Out-glitters *Waller*, and ev'n dazzles *Donne*.
Both of 'em, to *Augustus*, leave the Field;
Like *Lepidus* and *Anthony*, they yield.
He triumphs! their triumv'racy of Rays
Unite in *Cowley* and compound his blaze.

Poetical POVERTY. 1667. *To* C.M.D.

POverty, I, like Small Drink, hate;
  Yet 'tis, alas! the *Poet's* Fate.
And *Want* is such a stingey Crime,
It has no good excuse but *Rhyme*.
Yet here some comfort is exprest,
Poor, tho we be, the Poor are blest.
A favour granted by the *Church*,
To leave poor *Poets* in the lurch.
But they revenge this want of *Alms*,
By making her no better *Psalms*.
Who would make others sweetly chant,
And sigh themselves away for want?
As *Poets* shrivel'd *Guts* should be
Lute-strings for others Melody;
Thus *Nightingals* haste on their death,
By lavishing their sweet-tun'd Breath.
Those who rhyme on, and nothing get,
Ink may be call'd their *mortal Sweat*.
And every *Copy* that's so writ,
May be esteem'd their *Winding-sheet*.

Which

Which makes me to this Thought aſſent,
Poets did *Paper* firſt invent;
Whoſe prompting Wants did firſt begin
Such *Rags* to lap his Verſes in.

The Churching-FEAST. 1667.

To Sir Clifford Clifton, *for a Fat Doe.*

THO I kiſs without **Wit** or **Fear**,
 And get two *Children* in a year,
What is that to your harmleſs *Deer?*

Muſt one dye for each *Brat* of mine,
As tho my *Cod-piece* were a *Shrine ?*
Or *Priapus* again divine?

Such Bounty if you do not ſhun
It will diſ-park your *Hodſack* ſoon;
For each *Buck* is by me out-done.

If ſtill we both ſo forward be,
You'l find it a Neceſſity
To geld your Gifts as well as me.

If ſome do not for me this Knack,
I, like the *Mountebank,* may crack,
How that my *leaping* breaks my *Back.*

Let no man mock at what is writ;
To ſhew my Poverty is fit;
For *Want's* a ſpecial ſign of *Wit.*

Nor

Nor do thefe my Pretences cheat,
But their good Fortunes feek to get,
Who *Ballads* fing at Doors for *Meat.*

Then I may boaft *Apollo's* Skill,
If now a *fat Doe* I can kill
With th' feather'd *Arrow* of my *Quill.*

To *Orpheus* Fame I'll then afpire,
If one dance now to my defire,
Charm'd by the twangings of my *Lyre.*

A Midnight's R A P S O D Y   1668.

Upon my dear W. *at the point of Death.*

Dark time, alas! when both the light
    Of Heaven, and my fad Soul, have ta'n their
    And both intomb'd in deepeft night!   (flight,

Dejected Mufe! how canft thou think
To look or write, when th' *Eyes of Heav'n* do wink,
    And *Paper* looks it felf like *Ink ?*

Lord! but increafe my inward Sight ;
Thou who from *Chaos* didft create a *Light* ;
    One Smile from thee can gild my *Night.*

A *Night !* that foils the brighteft Ray
O'th' *Moon,* and clouds the cleareft Beam of *Day* ;
    Yet will thy fmalleft Glance obey.

Behold

Behold the courteous Queen of *Night*
's pleas'd to lend a *Ray*, by whofe kind light,
   Although wept blind, I now can write.

Hark how her pretty fmall ones cry!
And who can doubt that Heaven will deny
   Thofe Tears would *Marbles* mollifie?

My Pray'r, methinks, more fwiftly flies,
Born on the *Pinnions* of their purer Cries;
   Which court at once, and fcale the Skies.

Sleep then, fad Eyes; do not defpair
When next you ope to find th' effects of Pray'r;
   For Heav'n was hers, fhe Heaven's care.

Awake again! this fadly fhows
That falling Drops not always bring Repofe;
   Nor will Streams let my *Flood-gates* clofe.

My Grief flows with a conftant Tide,
Which does the *Ocean*'s fhallow Ebbs deride,
   And fwell'd does o're my *Eye-banks* glide.

Not yet wept dry! my Tears increafe!
After fuch *Show'rs* methinks this *Rain* fhould ceafe;
   Yet *Griefs*, like *Heat*, new *Vapours* raife.

Mix'd with my *Ink* let my Tears run;
And let thy holy Spirit move thereon,
   To make a facred *Helicon*.

                  Which

Which, like to *Jordan* then shall be,
And cleanse the stains of injur'd *Poetry,*
Too long defil'd with *Leprosie.*

'Tis fit alone to sing thy praise,
Thou who canst only give immortal *Bays,*
And us above our *Fancies* raise.

HOPE RUIN'D. 1668.

Upon the Death of the Right Honourable the Lady
Mary Mannors, *youngest Daughter to the No-*
ble House of Rutland.

SO long I staid (in vain, alas!) to try
   If other *Tributes* than those from the Eye,
Would have been offer'd at her *Virgin-Shrine* ;
But must, it seems, begin with this of mine.
Let others *Marble* give her *Tomb* to grace ;
It will my Glory be to pave the place.
Tho their bright *Torches* on her *Herse* must shine ;
'Tis Honour that this twinckling *Lamp* of mine
Did glimmer first : so does *Aurora* run,
As Usher to the Lord of Wit, the *Sun.*
When *Church* doors are shut up, true Pray'rs may
Though they be offer'd up in *Cottages.*   (please
But yet, methinks, 'tis odd to cherish Woes ;
Verse quickens Grief that is but flat in Prose.
Ingenious Lines but too much deck an Herse,
And briny Tears pickle up Grief in Verse.
Yet 'tis our Fate here ; who like Merchants lose
Our Treasures first, and then proclaim our Woes.
                                He

Her *Actions* were *Examples*; so that still
Those *Ladies* that don't practice her do ill.
She did excell the strictest *Cloister'd Saint*;
Affected *Purity* is worse than *Paint*.
And now she's gone, if *Poets* will declare,
And tell what Beauties other *Ladies* are,
They must get Praises from her *parts*, and tell
These *Coral Lips*, almost like hers, do swell;
Those *Eyes* resemble hers, that *Ladies* face
Has her sweet Features, this her winning Grace.
Each piece of hers makes perfect and compleat:
Thus a *King's* Ruines make ten thousand great.
So when the *Sun* is set, the *Queen* of *Night*
Borrows her shining Glory from his Light.
Sad Fate! thus when a *Rose-tree* dies at foot,
A croud of Beauties perish with the Root.
Let none then blame our Grief; 'tis not for one,
But for the Ruines of a *Million*.

The Early SPRING. 1669.

Upon the immature Death of my honoured Friend
Theophilus Parkyns, *Esq*;

TO lay this precious *Dust*, which the rough hours
  Of *March* did cause, *April* now pours
    It self away in Showers:
    Such Drops produce a Spring,
  And thus enable us to bring
These flow'rs, alas! which on his Herse we fling.

The

The *Muses Gardens* cannot yield supplies
   If we his worth should justly prize,
      Eden would scarce suffice :
      Nor could *Arabia* yield
   From out her parcht and spicy Field,
Odours and *Gums* enow his *Pile* to build.

Altho this *Fun'ral-charge* may prove too deep
   For any Poet's brains to keep;
      Yet we, alas, can weep!
      This *Deluge* of our Eyes
   May help to make his *Coffin* rise,
Like *Noah's Ark*, and raise it to the Skies.

When we have wept all this, we may have fears,
   The *Briny Ocean* of our tears
      Not half enough appears :
      For judge by what we lost,
   (Out *Country's* nay our *Nation's* boast)
If tears, or words can give sufficient cost.

How beautiful each look, each line of's Face?
   Each limb, each motion had a grace;
      Nature in him did place
      What either Sex thinks rare ;
   Tall, and yet lovely ; strong yet fair ;
Venus and *Mars* in him compounded were.

Tho *Nature* to his *Body* was so kind ;
   Yet not content, he sought to find
      The beauties of the *Mind*,

At all perfections vies ;
Charming his Looks as *Ladies* Eyes ;
Bold as young *Heroes,* as old *Doctors,* wife.

His powr'ful Wit had fuch an Empire gain'd ;
It every Subject could command,
And all its Foes withftand.
Fro th' Schools it firft did come ;
As conq'ring *Cæsar* did from *Rome,*
'Till ftrong enough to rule its native home.

He who had gone fo far, might well have ftaid ;
But like a man that thrives o'th Trade,
He further progrefs made :
Like Rich men he fought more ;
Tho he had treafures heap'd in ftore,
Yet free from pride, he thought himfelf but poor.

Death did, alas, all thefe fair hopes betray ;
As Bloffoms in a Frofty day.
Drop from a *Tree* in *May.*
His *Autumn* was not flow ;
And yet furpriz'd by *Winter* fo,
His fruit lyes bury'd now in *Sheets of Snow.*

Tho whilft alive we fcarcely faw him right ;
His worth will now come more in fight :
As *Stars* fhine moft by night.
Why then fhould foolifh I,
To raife his fame thus vainly try,
When things eternal can themfelves fupply ?

R   The

The F R I E N D. 1669.

Epitaph upon Roger Waldron, *Esquire.*

R Eader, what pale cold Gueſt
    Under this *ſpeaking Stone* does reſt,
Is by theſe faithful lines expreſt.

One of an ancient *Name,*
    Who left as full and clear a fame
To's *Children,* as fro's *Grandſires* came.

Nature to him did lend
    A Heart, that knew no other end,
But how to love, and ſerve his Friend.

His humour rightly plac'd,
    And ſo by converſation grac'd ;
It, *manna* like, did pleaſe each Taſt.

This is no flatt'ring dreſs;
    For Envy's ſelf muſt needs confeſs
Truth and a *Friend* could ſay no leſs.

Y O R K. 1670.

A Prologue for a Company of Players *leaving* London
for York, *upon their firſt appearance.*

M Ethinks you all look here, as you would know
    Why we left *London* to attend on you.

I' th' firſt place, we could ſtay no longer there,
Becauſe new *Playes* were both ſo bad, and dear,
We could not thrive o'th' trade : for each Wit now
Regards far more his *Belly,* than his *Brow.*
The ſecond thing that made us to retire,
Alas, the *Mercer's* Books eſcap'd the *Fire !*
The third, the *Gallants* were ſo worn, they muſt
Not ſee a *Play,* unleſs it were on truſt :
But with us *Infidels* that would not do ;
Our *Pit,* and Women then they'd *enter* too,
And no *admittance* pay : But we were loth
----*Cuckolds* to be, and *Beggars* both.

But the grand mover of our forc'd retreat ;
We were inſpir'd by *Prophecies* and *Fate.*
Tho *London* the *Metropolis* be known ;
York has the grandeur in reverſion.
And *Shipton's Prophecies* may now prove true ;
Since we have *London* left to wait on you.

Epilogue.

MEre thanks make but a ſlender ſhew,
When for great favours more are due ;
Yet, Gentlemen, they're all we have for you.

But weel indeavour to repay
The Time, the Coin you caſt away ;
Wee'l tell you how, if you but pleaſe to ſtay.

For thoſe three hours you here ſhall ſit ;
Wee'l give you Scenes of Mirth, and Wit ;
Such as the *Poet* ne'r in three Months writ.

K 2 Then

Then with our *Jewels* we devise
To pay the Ladies back that prize,
Which we each day shall purchase from their Eyes.

Yet here we have a hard *Task* met:
Tho ours were right, and richly set,
Ladies, your Eyes would make 'em counterfeit.

Our gen'rous freeness then to show;
For th' *Money* you on us bestow,
Wee'l spend it all amongst you e're we go.

The VILLIERS. 1671.

To my honour'd Friend, Sir George Villiers, *Bar.*

YOU from the *Vulgar* are far off remov'd,
  Where 'tis disparagement ev'n to be lov'd.
Yet as we see the greater *Worlds* bright eye
Warms all below, whilst it does move on high;
So, you forget the State to which you're born;
Your goodness pardons what your height may scorn.
And yet 'tis true that to your self you owe
Th' officious troubles their respects bestow.
For were you but less worthy, or more proud,
You'd soon be free from the adoring croud.
But such attractive Virtues take their place
Alwayes in some of your illustrious Race;
That in each Age Fame does 'em justly sing
True *Favrites* to their *Country*, or their *King.*
A glorious truth! since from your *Grandsire* came
He (who was justly both) great *Buckingham.*

You

*·Your *Brooksby* boaſts, we her may juſtly bleſs
For th' honour o' th' laſt age, the love of this.
And yet here ſprings a doubt, whether's more due,
This boaſt to your brave *Anceſtors*, or you.
You who reflect their worth, and makes us ſee
Both what they were, and what your *Son* will be.

  * Where *Bucking.* was born ; one of Sir *G.V.* his Lordſhips.

The VALENTINE. 1671.

To Mrs. J. M. *beſtowing a Preſent in a Letter.*

DID not ſufficiently my glory ſhine,
   When you acknowledg'd me your *Valentine?*
But you muſt add new *Trophies* to your praiſe,
And make that *Vaſſal* rich you pleas'd to raiſe?
Thus generous *Princes*, when their pow'rs they ſhow,
They *Titles* firſt, and then *Eſtates* beſtow.
Madam, in this with *Heav'n* you ſhare renown ;
Which makes a *Saint*, and after gives a *Crown.*
Your coſtly gift though too too rich before,
Yet you with richer lines have gilded o're,
Lines, where each word, nay letter may be fit,
To prove a *Cordial* to decaying Wit.
A favour which at once I cannot know ;
Since at each reading I ſee new ones grow :
Like th' *Orange-Tree*, whoſe fruit at once, and bloom
Bleſſes this Seaſon, and the next to come.
But we, alas, who're only rich in dreams
Of *Golden Sands*, that pave *Pactolus* Streams.
Yet ſadly find (when ſeriouſly we think)
No *Sand* but *Pinduſt*, and no *Stream* but *Ink* ;

We

We can make no returns but thanks, and thofe
Would found too flat, if only dreft in *Profe.*
Your favour was obliging to excefs ;
'Tis fit my Gratitude fhould be no lefs.
And no expreffions here can act that part,
Unlefs they be extracted from the heart.
Neither can thefe their purpofes obtain,
If not in *Verfe,* th' *Elixir* of the *Brain.*
Thus, *Madam,* when you have my chiefeft ftore
Of brain, and heart, tis vain to offer more.

DANGEROUS SAFETY. 1671.

To the Honourable Mrs. Chaworth.

SOL (tho his *Throne* be in the *Skies*)
    Vouchfafes the courtfhip of our *Eyes.*
We are as much oblig'd to you,
Bleft with the favour of your view.
And tho from us you're fo much rais'd,
That it's below you to be prais'd;
Yet 'tis our duty to admire,
And honour you without defire.
Our *Lownefs* guards us ; and our fhare
Of fafety comes from our *Defpair.*
Our thoughts are daunted at your fight:
Thus *falvage Beafts* are tam'd with *Light.*
Such fainting hopes cannot fucceed ;
Our thoughts againft our felves we breed :
|| Poor *Græcians* thus inflaved were
By *Children,* which themfelves did bear.
The two-edg'd Sword of your bright Eyes
Keeps back the croud of amorous fighs.

|| A Tribute of
their children
whence are
made the *Spa-
chi* and *Ja-
nizaries,* the
ftrength of the
Turks.

You'l

Your *Rofes*, and your *Lillies* are
Safe-fenc'd againft'prefumptuous Air.
We know your Virtues, and we prize
The charming Glories of your Eyes;
But this can no more good bequeath,
Than *Wine* to *Perfons* doom'd to death :
Like tortur'd *Souls*, who know that blifs
Which they're, alas, condemn'd to mifs.

The RESCUE. 1672.

To Mrs. D. C. Whofe name being left after drawing Valentines and caft into the Fire, was fnatcht out.

FOrtune, that does the World fubdue,
    Submits her Empire here to you.
Your fmiles can fix her changing ftate,
And fpight of her can blifs create.
Henceforth you will more courted be,
And have more *Altars* far than fhe.
You need not her Advancements mind,
No more than *Light* to be refin'd.
Compoft is vain for your rich *Soil* ;
Your *Di'mond* fhines without a *foil* ;
And you have fuch an awful flame,
She durft not meddle with your *Name.*
Which fcorn'd her Laws, and would not be
Subfervient to her *Lottery.*
She rag'd with fury at the flight,   *Nebuchado-*
Aping the *Syrian Tyrant*'s fpite ;   *nezer.*
That did to flames thofe Perfons vow,
Who would not to his *Idol* bow.

K 4

I like

I, like the *Angel*, did aspire,
Your *Name* to rescue from the fire.
My Zeal succeeded for your *Name*;
But I, alas, caught all the flame!
A meaner off'ring thus suffic'd,
And *Isaac* was not sacrific'd.

The REFORMADO. 1672.

*Upon a certain Levite who had tryed many Sects,
writing bald Acrosticks against Mr. R.W.*

INlighten'd by his fiery rant,
  I find out *George*, but not the *Saint*.
His Idle Phrensie makes it ghest,
Tho not inspir'd, he is possest.
The ancient *Jews* for cure did play,
And *Fiend* at *Musick* fled away.
But here, alas, our modern *Jew*
Is both the *Fiend*, and *Fidler* too.

Stumbling in his *Acrostick* way,
Look how his *Muses* feet are splay.
From letter they to letter stride:
As *Cripples* upon *Crutches* ride.
George, the fierce *Dogril*, tortures *Verse*,
'Till every *Sheet* becomes an *Herse*.
For as that *Tyrant's* cruel wit
Made each man's legs his *Bed-stead* fit:
So here's a foot rackt to reach G,
And here's one lopt to size with D.

Procrustes.

When

When Verse does in *Acrosticks* lie,
The tortur'd sense lies gasping by.
Look but with what a painful pride,
His *Pegasus* does trammel'd ride.
Like *Baker's* Palfry thorough pac'd;
An *Issachar* 'twixt *Panniers* plac'd.
But he pretends to *Helicon*,
As *Priest* of the *Prophetick Tun.*
For as of old, the *Delphian Knave*,
Inspir'd fro' th' hole of *Sybil's Cave*,
With glowing Cheeks and staring Eyes
Half mad did from the *Tripos* rise;
And then with odd phrenetick zeal
The fates of Mortals did reveal:
So when prophetick *George* does come
From sage *Eliza's lower room;*
Inspir'd with false outragious zeal,
With brains and cheeks red hot with Ale,
Having first set his *Mouth* to *Bung;*
His chanting *Oracles* are sung.

Deep *George* in ancient *Saws* delights;
A *Grecian* only in their *Rites.*
With pious fictions, impious jests,
And *Revels* fitting *Cibel's* Priests,
Reeling from *Bacchanalian* feasts.

If old *Pythagoras* rule hold true,
How each soul transmigrates a new;
That unfledg'd *Muse* in former times
Which flutter'd into *Hopkin's* Rhymes,
Being lured now to *George* his use,
Seems transmigrated to a *Goose.*

But

But such a *Goose* whose gagling bawl,
Is hir'd to serve the *Capitol.*
His Faith, as well as Wit, is known
To've suffer'd *Transmigration* :
For having learnt the *Garb* and *Caw,*
It transmigrated to a *Daw.*
And *Jack-daw*-like in *Church* did rest,
Till the foul Bird defil'd its nest.
Then, *Dormouse* like, made its repair,⎫
T' a *Meeting-house,* with twilight pray'r,⎬
And roosted in a *Cobler's Chair;* ⎭
Till to a *Drake* it did arrive,
And with the *Dipper* learnt to dive.
Then *Raven*-like the *Air* did coast,
And hover'd over *Cromwel's Host;*
Incouraging that *Tyrant's* crime,
Its *Feathers* took a deeper grime.
Yet, as old *Nick* would fain seem white,
To ape the glorious Sons of light;
So *George* in *Surplice* now does lurk, ⎫
Gaining this Title for his work, ⎬
George- Bajazet the *Christian Turk.* ⎭

The CONTEST. 1673.
Upon the death of my dear S. Mrs. M.S.

DEar precious Soul! tho now thou shin'st more bright
Than new born *Phœbus,* swath'd about with light ;
Accept this gloomy, tho free Sacrifice ;
If it can pierce the mounting Clouds of Sighs.
My Grief, and Love (like two fierce storms) contest,
And raise an Earthquake in my trembling breast,

Both

Both ftrive for maftery, yet neither yield ;
Grief fometimes,and Love fometimes gains the Field;
As two ftout *Mutineers* in *Fortrefs* penn'd,
Ruine that Place by ftrife, they fhould defend.

O! that our Souls, of a cœleftial Race,
And neither circumfcrib'd to time or place ;   (arts
Should (whilft they're clog'd with flefh) not have the
T' obey the motions of our loving Hearts ;
Each other (tho at diftances) to greet,
And at each moment in imbraces meet.
But we fhall meet e're long, tho I be flow,
And with mine unfledg'd Pinnions ftay below.
Thy Soul (being born on glorious Angels wings)
And guided by thofe bright and friendly things,
Did get the ftart, and fly to Heav'n before me,
Altho I fet out fourteen years before thee.
But none can be the glorious *Bridegroom's Gueft*,
Unlefs accouter'd for the *Wedding-Feaft*.
They're thruft, alas, as bold *Pretenders* thence,
Who glitter not in robes of *Innocence* ;
Shine not in *Chaftity, Devotion, Peace,*
Humility, and fuch like Gems as thefe.

Thou having gain'd thofe *Ornaments* before,
And brought by *Angels* as a *fitting Gueft* ;
  Saint Peter open'd foon the *fhining Door*,
And gladly let thee in amongft the reft.

The

The RICH PURCHASE. 1673.

To the honourable Mrs. Chaworth, *commanding two of my Tragedies.*

THE *Town*'s applaufe is but a dream ;
   You are my *Theater*, and *Theme.*
'Tis you that kindle *Fancies* fire ;
Whofe very fmile does Wit infpire.
The *Mufes*, nay the *Graces* too,
Were only *dusky Types* of you.
More influence does in one Eye
Of yours, than whole *Apollo* lye.
And you muft merit moft efteem ;
Who make thofe *Poets*, that make him.
That Wit we labour for with pain,
More happy you by *Nature* gain.
And *Virtue* which from *Rules* we own,
Is, *Madam*, your *Complexion.*
Our blifs you only muft create ;
If we can faintly imitate.
But that will be as hardly done,
As for fmall *Lamps* t'out-fhine the *Sun.*
Yet Heav'n will thofe *Devoto*'s fit
For glory, that but aim at it :
Thus I may gain by giving praife ;
And off'ring *Lawrels*, purchafe *Bays.*

POE-

POETICAL PLENTY 1673.

To my good friend Mr. Ar. Lomax, saying, I had not
yet learn'd to ballance my Expences, nor either of
us guilty of hoarding Money.

BAllance *Expences Friend!* sure thou dost ghess
I'm damnably given to excess,
Or *Purse* than *Stomack* less:
Neither's too great, I swear;
Yet I might purchase better chear,
If I that knack of *Drinking* could forbear.

I'le rather learn the Science how to steal,
Than be prescribed for my Meal
Thin broath and *Racks* of Veal.
I'm yet in no such strait,
Besieged by my wants, or fate,
Like sterv'd-out *Towns*, to eat, and drink by weight.

'Tis Tyranny to any free-born heart,
To be confined to a *quart*;
I'le rather have no part.
Set-diet shews a want,
And danger too; since *Casuists* grant
Our Grandam *Eve* sin'd chiefly by *restraint.*

My self to famish to increase my store,
Is to take pains how to be poor;
I'le rather run o'th' Score.
For I would rather fear
Grim Judges and their *Sentence* hear,
Than be my self my *Executioner.*

If

If thou'rt not rich, thou would'ft not Fates obey,
Who fet thee in a ready way,
But led me quite aftray :
For *Megs*, with tempting light,
(Which are the *Mufes*, as fome write)
Dazled mine Eyes, and did miflead me quite.

Thefe *Dalila's* they tempted out mine Eyes,
And made me grope like foolifh Boys,
For praife and *Wreaths*, mere Toys !
When that care (fome will fay)
If but turn'd downwards (the right way)
Had digg'd up *Gold*, as foon as pluck't the *Bay*.

But fam'd *Parnaffus*, and the Silver ftream
Of too-bewitching *Hippocrene*,
Me from thofe thoughts did wean :
They, like fome *Fairy Land*,
Or like fcortch'd *Affrick* flatt'ring ftand.
With pleafant Shores, but full of barren Sand.

'Tis true, we pleafe our Fancies, and can tow'r,
Like chirping *Larks* after a fhower;
But 'tis not in our power
In that ftate to remain ;
But to the Earth we fall again,
Eying the *Sun's* bright *Gold*, we ne'r obtain.

Yet for all this, I muft the *Mufes* love ;
Conftrain'd by fome odd Pow'r above,
Tho they unkindly prove:
Inflav'd thus by our Fate
Is our mad Sex, that cannot hate
Woman, that ruin'd firft our happy ftate.

Thefe

Those sweet *Devourers* by our selves are nurst :
   As from his side old *Adam* first
     Gave what him after curst.
     Each *Poet Adam* is,
   His *Muse* an *Eve*, who makes him miss,
With false pretences tempting him from bliss.

Thou Damn'd inchanting *Wealth*, alluring *Hagg* !
   Keep in thy smoth'ring *Hell*, thy *Bag*,
     And make not me thy brag.
     Whilst I but thought of thee ;
   Such is thy devillish *Witchery*,
I was infected with thy *Heresie*.

Wouldst thou turn me a *Rebel* ? have me seen
   To take up Arms against my *Queen* ?
     Hold, hold, my swelling *Spleen* !
     Wouldst stop my *Muses Song* ?
   Like that base *Wretch*, who did the wrong
To *Philomel*, and then cut out her tongue ?

Pardon *Apollo*, and you *Muses nine* ;
   Tho your *Hill*'s bare it is a sign
     It does infold a *Mine*.
     Yet, fool, how was I craz'd,
   Like silly *Conjurers*, amaz'd
With *Apparitions*, that my self had rais'd ?

Poets are counted poor ; 'tis true ; but know
   They riches have, they will not show ;
     Deep *Rivers* silent flow.
     There is a *Place* they call,
   At *Rome*, Saint *Peter*'s *Hospital*,
And yet the *Pots* and *Dishes Silver* all.

               They

They have no shining *Oar*, no pleasing *Chink* ;
  Yet find in *Verse* a *sweeter clink* ,
    And glitter in their *Ink.*
     Such wealth will not deny
  Them *Wings*, with *Gold* they cannot fly,
Tis th' heavi'st *Metal*, and with *Dirt* mustlye.

Gold is the dross, and *Wit* the precious *Oar* ;
  Whilst *Poets* do injoy that store,
    How can they be call'd poor ?
     This tho the World gain-say ;
  It, like bad *Chymists* throws away
The purer *Metal* keeping the *Allay.*

Apollo's so attractive, some we see
  Would leave their *Infidelity.*
    And real *Converts* be :
     They gladly would compound,
  And now his *Temples* do surround :
Thus *Christian Churches* with the *Turks* are found.

Such *Hereticks*, who have been so profane ;
  All their devotion will be vain
    Before his Sacred *Fane*:
     For none such can be gheft
  Worthy to be *Apollo*'s *Priest* ;
Some whining *Clerk*, or *Deacon* at the best.

Then let us charily keep close our Skill,
  As they do all their Treasure still ;
    Soon change with us they will :

                    Else

Elſe when they come to dye,
How will they get an *Elegy* ?
For *Poets* when unpaid, will never lye.

The N E W - Y E A R 'S G I F T. 1674.
To the honourable Mrs. Chaworth.

COME, great *Apollo* now, and ſhew thy might ;
Thou glorious *Patron* both of *Wit* and *Light.*
From thoſe two gifts, the greateſt comfort's hurl'd,
Both on the greater, and the leſſer *World.*
Advance ſome *Preſent* worthy of her Eyes ;
But that will quite impoveriſh thy *Skies.*
And yet thou may'ſt thoſe Treaſures ſafely ſpare,
Since ſhe'l once bring more Beauties than are there.
Yet keep 'em to thy ſelf, ſo thou'lt beſtow
Some of thoſe treaſures, that thou mak'ſt below.
  Gold is thy work, tho, not as *Dryden* ſaid,
When under *Turfs* to hatch by *Indians* laid.
The gheſs this way more probably is told ;
For when thou pour'ſt on earth thy *molten Gold;*
(Which ev'ry night aſcends to thee again)
Gold is the *Droſs,* that does below remain,
  The *Rocks* of *Ormus,* and of *Bengelay,*
In whoſe dark *Caves Jewels* create a day ;
Thou mak'ſt thoſe *Gems* (whoſe light thy luſtre mocks)
Fine exudations of thoſe pregnant *Rocks* ?
Thy *Rayes* contracted into drops, are found
The cauſe o' th' luſtre of the *Diamond.*
When thou, for thy refreſhures every night,
Dives to imbrace thy beauties *Amphitrite;*
                L   Thoſe

Those pleasant *Coral Groves* i'th' *Deeps* below,
Blest by thy smiles obtain their tincture so.
And glitt'ring *Pearls*, fixt on the roots of *Rocks*,
Are dew-drops shaken from thy shining *Locks*.

From those bright *Pearls* either a *Neck-lace* spare,
Which by her *Skin* improv'd, may turn more fair:
Or from those *Diamonds* vouchsafe supplies;
Which will gain brighter lustre from her *Eyes*:
At which some of the brightest sham'd will grow,
And by their blushes turn to *Rubies* so:
Or with some *Coral branches* be but kind,
And in her *Lips* they'l richer Scarlet find:
Or grant me *Saphires*, and their fainter stayns
Shall take a purer *Azure* from her *Veins*.
Or if to give them all thou'lt be so kind;
They'l yield to th' treasures of her richer *Mind*.

At these great truths *Apollo*, 'sham'd, withdrew;
Sham'd to be baffled and out-shin'd by you:
His treasures, and his favours now denies.
But, *Madam*, I hope greater from your Eyes.
The heavenly pow'rs thus their acceptance show
Of Duties, by the Blessings they bestow.
And tho your *merits* to such heights are rais'd, ⎫
That my weak Eyes to see them are amaz'd, ⎬
You've too much light not to be seen and prais'd. ⎭
Altho I am unfit your praise to write,
Some dusky gleams flash from the darkest night.
Virtue's adorn'd enough with Native rayes,
Needing no garnish from a Poet's praise;
Yet just repute may add to Virtues height:
As curious *Pictures* are advanc'd by *light*.

Your

Your smiles I crave not, only beg a glance,
Since honour'd by your *Father's* countenance ;
That *noble Lord* ! to whom such fame is due
From all the *World*, because he gave it you.
In whom he paid more than himself did cost ;
Tho from his Blood great *Monarchs* make their boast
Judge of this truth since the *Lancastrian* Line
Vouchsaf'd its glorious beams with his to joyn.
Its *Rose*, tho crimson'd with its *native flood*,
Yet took rich tinctures from *Cadurcis blood*. *Vid. Heylins*
For tis a doubt, whether more fame is due, *Cosmogr.pag.*
To come from *Kings*, or *Kings* to come from you.
  Since *Blessings* by that *Match* did so abound ;
That many *Princes* sprung from thence were *crown'd* ;
I must beg pardon to presume it due
For some of them to give a *Crown* to you.

BEAUTIES PERIPHRASIS. 1674.

To Mrs. E. W.

MY *Muse*, more happy far than I,
      Has long my *Mistris Hand-maid* been,
Us'd to unlace, unpin, untye,
      And has all her *Perfections* seen.

On *New-years* day I spy'd my *Madam* ;
      She and the Year both in their prime,
More fresh, than was the *Miss* of *Adam*
Sprung from the *Maiden-head* of *Time*.

Her *Garments* I will firſt diſcloſe ;
    Then naked lay my bluſhing *Queen*,
The ſame procedure has the *Roſe* ;
    Firſt *Leaves*, and then the *Bud* is ſeen.

Her *Hoods* ſometimes her Beauties hide ;
    Which cuſtom may be well allow'd :
Since *Sol's* bright *Face* in all his pride,
    Is often hid beyond a *Cloud.*

Her *Viſard-mask,* that hides her face,
    Declares more cruelty than ſtate ;
She looks as *Beauty Priſoner* was,
    And peeping through a double *grate.*

Amongſt her *Curls* ſhe *Jewels* wears,
    All glittering with thoſe ſhining *drops* :
Which like *Aurora's pearly Tears,*
    Sit trembling on the *Lillies* tops.

If we conſider worth or ſtate ;
    The *Diamond neck-lace* that ſhe wears,
May challenge *Ariadne's* fate,
    And turn into a *wreath of Stars.*

Her coſtly *Points* by *Artiſts* fram'd,
    Like *Wings* of *Cherubims* imbrace
Her ſwelling *Breaſts* ; which once I nam'd
    (Unjuſtly tho) the *Mercy-place.*

Her *Gowns,* tho rich, and worthy pride,
    Lock up the beauties of her youth :
Like cloudy *Parables* that hide
    The glorious majeſty of *Truth.*

                                   Her

Her *Gloves* are like the tender *Rind*
    Of that rare *Plant*, that fweateth *Balm*,
The truth of this you'd quickly find,
    If you but kift her *melting Palm.*

Through *fcarlet-ftockins* fhines her *Skin* :
    Light pierces thus *red-painted Glaffes.*
Ten fhining *Pearls* inclos'd within,
    Are lockt up in thofe *ruby Cafes.*

Her *Shoos* with envy I did prize,
    And wifh'd my felf be fo grac'd ;
Stor'd with two pair of open *Eyes*,
    For tempting objects rightly plac'd.

Her envious *Smock* tho hid my blifs :
    Thus *Snow* ftrikes earneft gazers blind ;
All may be feen when thaw'd it is
    By *Love*, that *Sun fhine* of the *Mind.*

Her *Beauties* are cloath'd o're with light,
    Not here expos'd to wild defires ;
Such thoughts, the beams of vertue fright :
    As rav'nous *Beafts* retreat from *fires.*

Her *Hair* may juftly make her prouder
    Than *Queens* who to their *Crowns* were born;
And looks when candy'd o're with powder,
    Like *Sun-beams* in a *rimy morn'.*

A curious chryftal *prop* (*her Nofe*)
    Supports the *Arches* of her *Skies.*
Her *Front* the *chryftalline Heaven* fhows,
    Studded with fhining *Stars*, her *Eyes.*

Each

Each *Cheek* like to a *Roseal Grove,*
    Where thousand *Cupids* sporting lye ;
Whetting their several *Darts* of Love ;
    Her *Brows* the *Bows* from whence they flye.

Her *simpring Mouth* such charms declare,
    Which *Rhetorick* never could produce ;
Her *Lips,* like *full-ripe Cherries,* are
    Preserv'd in their own natural *Juyce.*

Her *Breath* more sweet than *perfum'd gales,*
    That from *Arabian Gardens* blow ;
Or those which sweep the *Indian Vales,*
    Where *Jasmins* in their vigours grow.

Such treasures of her Breath and Tongue,
    Ought not to be too much expos'd ;
Hence Fate, to bulwark them from wrong,
    With double fence of *Pearls* inclos'd.

Her *Shoulders Beauty's Atlas* are,
    But coverd with a purer *Snow* ;
And far a richer burden bear
    Of Beauties, and of Glories too.

Her *Breasts* a pair of *Ivory Bowls,*
    With *Biasses* of *Rubies* nail'd :
Or else two whitest *Paper-scrouls,*
    Which *Nature* had with *red-wax* seal'd.

Beneath those *Hills* a *Valley* spread ;
    Where *Violets* and *Lillies* strove ;
Through which a perfum'd *Path* did lead,
    Directing to th' *Elisian Grove.*

Her

Her *Back-fide* two ound fnowy *Mountains*,
 Which 'twixt 'em did a *Valley* hide;
In which did fpring a pair of *Fountains*,
 Where *Gold* and *Silver* ftreams did glide.

Her *Knees*, I thofe rare *Hinges* named,
 On which this beauteous *Fabrick* mov'd;
Her *Thighs*, the *Columns* ftrongly framed
 On which my ftately *Temple* ftood.

Thus have I vowed, fworn, protefted,
 To lift my *Miftris* to the Sky;
Yet, cruel fhe, thinks I but jefted;
 And, by my troth, Sirs, fo think I.

REPOSE. 1674.

To *Mr.* W. W. *of* Grantham.

NOT for the reafon others do,
 It is I now follicit you:
A jufter caufe defigns my choice;
It is for your fake, not your *Boyes.*
Excefs of ftudy does you wrong;
A *Bow* may break that's bent too long.
The Heav'nly *Bow* (whofe lafting ftuff,
Would make one think it ftrong enough)
Is not bent always, but allow'd
To be cas'd up within a *Cloud.*

Let none here mock at what is faid;
For *Archery* is there a *Trade.*

   L 4   *Dian.*

Dian, Apollo, Archers good ;
And *Cupid* is their *Robin Hood,*
Long fhining *Darts Apollo* fhoots ;
Th' *Antipodes,* and we his *Butts.*
Yet when 'tis night his *Bow* unbends,
And *Arrows* to his *Sifter* lends ;
Who buckles to't (her skill to fhow)
'Till fhe become the very *Bow.*
And when fhe's at the utmoft bent,
Her *Darts* with brighteft *Piles* are lent ;
Yet fhe by day refrefhment feeks.
Then *Cupid* moftly fhoots at *Pricks;*
And when at *Butts* the *motto* nicks.
Strange *marks-man,* who ne'r miffes aim,
Yet flacks his *ftring* at every Game.
Moifture, (that *heart-blood* of the *Earth*)
From whence all things derive their birth,
Shrinks fometimes to the Springs i' th' *Deep,*
That fo it may its vigours keep.
Sap (that *prolifick Sperm* of *Trees*)
Beftows its bleffings by degrees ;
Bloffoms and *Leaves* it gives i' th' *Spring;*
And does its fruit in *Autumn* bring ;
In *Winter* tho retires to th' *Deep,*
New ftrengths to gain or old to keep.
The *Soul* (that bright cœleftial *Gueft*)
Altho eternal, feeks for reft.
Nor can this *Eafe* be a difgrace ;
Since *Heav'n*'s the chiefeft refting place.

The

The GROVE. 1675.

Some thoughts dedicated to the Nymphs of the plea-
sant Grove at S. belonging to my most honour'd
Friend Peniston Whalley *Esq.*

How am I in an instant blest?
   This *Grove* affords some chearful Guest,
A stranger to my wounded breast.

But how can *Musick* there be found,
Where daunting cares have made a wound?
Yet breaking *Heart-strings* yield a found.

But now my *Crest-fall'n* thoughts aspire;
As *Saul's* black humours did retire,
Before the *twangs* of *David's* lire.

Verse has such charms, It can advance
A captive Soul from hellish Trance,
Can bridle *Dolphins*, make *Beasts* dance.

But stay, I doubt this boasted grace
Denies its rise from my dull layes ;
And owes its Being to this place.

As *Priests* of old were not inspir'd,
Their breasts with sacred heat ne'r fir'd,
'Till they into their *Groves* retir'd.

Nor came this Virtue from the *Trees*,
Nor from the *Prophet's Rapsodies*,
But from the *Neighb'ring Deities*.

None

None views this *Grove* but soon allows
It is a *Temple* roof'd with Boughs;
Where faithful *Lovers* pay their *Vows.*

And that betwixt the *Leaves,* those spaces
(Through which the prying *Sun-shine* passes)
Seem quarter'd *Panes* of *Chrystal* Glasses.

Then *Nature* here each year does bring
The sweet-tongu'd *Black-coats* of the *Spring,*
With other *Choristers* to sing.

Who to this service are ordain'd,
From its *Revenues* are maintain'd,
With *Berries* from the *Bushes* gain'd.

Yet if you take a neerer view,
The *Simile* will seem more true;
This *Temple* has its *Scriptures* too.

Upon the *Barks,* with curious slit,
Devotion is ingrav'd with Wit,
And by some *Goddess Fingers* writ.

Whose adoration, merit, fame,
Shall still inlarge, as does the *Name,*
Which *thrives* till it *out-grows* the *frame.*

Nor do the *Trees* confus'dly stand;
But *rank'd,* and *fil'd* as they were trayn'd
By the *Commanders* skilful hand.

Each

Each row of sturdy *Oaks* appears
Squadrons of *English Musketeers* ;
The *Acorns Shot, Leaves Bandileers.*

Those stands of *Ashes* strongly spread,
Like our stout *Pike men*, void of dread ;
With *Keys*, like *Fringe* about each *head.*

Here *Elms:* whose bending Boughs retain
The shapes of our old *Bows* in vain ;
Never to conquer *France* again.

Those *Aspen-trees*, like **French**, look high ;
As they would scale the very sky ;
Yet shake, whilst *English Elms* are by.

The *Willows* here like **Dutchmen** show ;
All sap, not good for *Pyke* or *Bow* ;
And only will by *Waters* grow.

Thrice happy *Trees*, where future times
(Not clouded with our present crimes)
Shall in their *Barks* read am'rous rhymes.

For who can greater Wit desire
Than that, which *Beauty* does inspire ?
Verse then is cloath'd in *Queens* attire.

It needs must be a happy sight,
The golden age did first delight
All Verse in *Rynds* of *Trees* to write.

Tho

Tho *Bayes* and *Lawrels* ſtill abound,
Nobler rewards will then be found ;
They'l with their *Ladies Names* be crown'd.

Each then muſt lofty *numbers* frame,
Whilſt ſhe thereto ſubſcribes her *Name* ;
'Twill be at once, *Reward* and *Theme.*

If I that happy fate could prove,
Incourag'd by thoſe Eyes I love ;
This ſhould out-vye *Dodona's Grove.*

But as I firſt with cares were croſt ;
Theſe thoughts have ſo my Soul ingroſt,
That I am in this *Laby'rinth* loſt.

When loe! as I did gaze about,
I ſaw a *Path*, which (without doubt)
As't leades them in, will lead me out.

With *Lady-Smocks*, and *Dayes-Eyes* white ;
The very *Path* they tread are bright *:*
So the *Sun's tracks* are *pav'd* with *Light.*

The RENT. 1675.

To the honourable Lady, Mrs. Chaworth.

Advice againſt envious Reports.

MY *Rent-day's* come, and I muſt pay.
  Nor muſt your plenty make me ſtay,
Leſt I grow poorer by delay.

For-

Forbearance but unkind appears;
And the poor *Tenant*'s juſteſt fears
May be deduc'd from long *Arrears.*

Whilſt either *Wit* or *Fancy* grows,
They're yours; but when depriv'd of thoſe,
I muſt be forc'd to pay in *Proſe.*

Decaying Farmers thus lament;
When their beſt *Stock,* and *Mony*'s ſpent,
Their very *Raggs* are ſeiz'd for *Rent.*

This is a *Quit-rent* yearly paid;
By which my *Title*'s ſurer made;
Th' *Eſtate* elſe may be forfeited.

Tho ſuch mean *Homages* you ſcorn;
Yet ſome, to noble Fortunes born,
Take nothing but a *Pepper-Corn.*

For theſe poor *Rhymes,* a pretty Cloak!
Words vaniſh with the breath th' are ſpoke:
Yet *Sacrifices* went in *Smoak.*

Truth's a great *Empreſs,* and will reign:
This *New-years-Gifts* pretence is vain;
It is not ſo much *Gift* as *gain.*

Thus our *Devotions,* when moſt hot,
Pay dues to Heav'n that needs 'em not;
We profit by the pious *Plot.*

Heav'n

Heaven at the *Heart* did ever aim,
Far more than at the coftly flame
Which from the *Sacred Altar* came.

Who would not fuch a *Goodnefs* truft,
That grateful is to worthlefs *Duft* ;
And makes them happy that are juft.

My *Duty* fuch procedures know ;
Since I in paying what I ow,
Purchafe that fame I would beftow.

But whence can I that *Parent* claim,
Either to give, or purchafe fame ?
Who nothing knows of it but name ?

Nor is it more than *fleeting Air* ;
Untill condens'd (by *Poet's* care)
To *Jewels* for each *Ladies* Ear.

Your worth fuch rich *Materials* brings,
Wherewith to make thofe precious things,
Fit both for *Ears,* and *Crowns* of *Kings.*

Difturb not then your felf, but fhun
Th' effects of *Envy,* for 'tis known
Obnoxious *Vapours* cloud the *Sun.*

Vertue's a *Piramid* of Light,
Attracting dazling Gazer's fight,
And envious *fhades* attend its *height*

With native *Balfam* eafe your pain
Tho *Skies* o'recaft, and turn to *Rain* ;
Thofe drops inrich the *Earth* with *Grain*

Tim

Time calms rough tempests, raging Seas?
No *Storms* can wreck an inward Peace:
Wrong'd Worth, like bruis'd Perfumes, increase.

Reports, like *Darts of Reed*, when shot
At a right *Breast-plate*, hurt it not;
You, Madam, have such *Armour* got.

There cannot be a surer fence
Than yours; whose *Guard* is *Innocence*,
And whose *Desires* are free'd from *sense*.

To raise the meanest doubt's a Sin:
She must the noblest *Trophies* win,
Whose *Fort*'s impregnable within.

In her a pow'r resistless lies,
Who bears *Artillery* in her Eyes;
And conquers *Death*'s self when she dies.

O L Y M P U S.   1675.

Spoken by Mrs. P. L. *to the right honourable the Lord
and Lady* Roos, *at* Belvoir, *before a Play; she
starting up, as rising from the dead.*

BLessings upon those Eyes! whose pow'rful shine
       Has open'd mine.
The *pointed raies* that from your *Glories* broke,
Like *Sun-beams*, glanc'd on me, and I awoke.
     Your rich intensive Light
Broke through the Clouds of Nature's deepest Night.
               Bright

Bright Twins ! your *Sun-like* power
Reviv'd a drooping *Flower*,
    And made it grow
From *Winding-sheets* and *Graves* of *Snow.*
May Smiles, Joyes, Loves, attend your sight;
For thence they gain their choicest light.
From you may ghastly Objects fly,
As gloomy shades fro' th' morning Sky.
    Nothing that can frightful be
To Innocence, or purity,
    Can in this *Orbe* appear ;
No more than darkness in the upper Sphear.
    If th' *Issue* of the Poets brain,
    Either were obscene, or vain ;
    We cleans'd his *Muse* ;
Like *muddy Carps* in *springing Stews.*
If in the *Cradle* any thing seem'd wild ;
    We *circumciz'd* the *Child* ;
    And tam'd its wanton rage :
    Thus *Priests* i' th' *Golden-Age*
    Only thought the *Sacrifice*
    Worthy to ascend the *Skies* ; .
When the *Smoak* vanish'd, and the *flame* did rise.
    Acceptance almost is our due;
    Since we are so devout for you.
    Consult this place, none can despair,
Since influenc'd from the *Noble*, and the *Fair.*
Your smiles, fair *Lady*, and most noble *Lord*,
    Must life to us afford.
    Shine from your lofty *Sphear*,
    Our blossomes soon will fruit appear.
Thus *Jove* and *Juno* on *Olympus* sate,
Smil'd on the *infant World*, and crown'd its fate.

A C T I V I T Y. 1676.

Upon the Death of Capt. Matt. Dale.

IN *Nature's* chiefeſt ſtrengths who would confide ?
Or in the choiceſt of her Gifts take pride ?
If either *Wit, Activity,* or *Truth,*
Wiſdom of *Age,* or *Jollity* of *Youth,*
Could have prevail'd with Death ; He had been ſafe;
Not living only in this *Epitaph.*

He with dull *Gravity* had ne'r to do ;
Diſcreet he was, yet a *good-fellow* too.
The ſtrongeſt fumes of *Wine* he could reſtrain,
And make 'em uſeful to his active Brain :
Thus ripening *dews* in pleaſant *Meads* are found ;
When noiſome *Miſts* ariſe in *boggy ground* ;
Unmanag'd Soils are worſe for fruitful ſhowers,
And bring forth *Weeds,* when *Gardens* ſmile with *Flow-*
His *Tongue* the motions of his *Heart* did tell :   (ers.
So th' *Clapper* ſhews the *Metal* of the *Bell.*
He made no difference 'twixt *Mine* and *Thine* ;
Fro' th' low-run *Age* he did thoſe *Dregs* refine :
Yet in his own *Concernments* was no *Tool*
For *Knaves* to work with, a *good-natur'd Fool* :
But, like the uſeful *Swiſs,* he could defend
His native *Cantons,* and aſſiſt his Friend.

In *Running* he did others ſo outvy,
'Tis wrong to him to ſay he did but fly.
Thoſe *myſtic Darts,* that are from *Objects* ſhot, He leapt at one
With ſlower motion to the *Sight* are got.   leap backward
And in his *Leaping,* his *Beholders* ſay,   and forward,
He did not *jump,* but *ſhot* himſelf away.   7 yards, now
                                                 mark't out in--
M   **His**

His *Back*, like *Indian-Bow*, with *Sinews* bent ;
And like an *Arrow*, from the *Jerk* he went.
Nature in one did ne'r more wonders show ;
Himself the *Archer, Arrow, String*, and *Bow*.
Nay, at his Death he practis'd o're this part ;
And did, in several Postures, try his Art.
First, to the Posture of the *Swede* he got,
And then from bended Knees his *Arrows* shot ;
With out-stretch'd *Arms* fro's *Breast* such *Darts* he drew,
Sherwood's fam'd *Bow-men*'s shafts they quite o're-flew.
Theirs only aim'd at *Sun* and *Moon* ! his high'r ;
Feather'd with *Angels Plumes*, and *Piles* of *fire* :
Nothing flyes swifter than *inflam'd Desire*.
Then *Death*'s convulsive *Cramps* his *Body* drew
To th' utmost bent, till it in pieces flew.
A *Bombard* thus o're-loaden, when 'tis broke,
Sends forth its dying groans in sighs of Smoak.
Th' infolded *Ball* tho, cloath'd in bright attire,
Elias-like, mounts in a *Coach* of *Fire*.

The HEROINE. 1676.

Upon the death of the right Honourable Frances
Countess of Rutland, &c.

NO heats of *Love*, nor thirsts of *Fame*,
    Did *Poet*'s mind e're more inflame
Than mine, to write great *Rutland*'s Name.

My meanness let no man despise ;
We know the smoak of *Sacrifice*,
That aim'd at *Heav'n*, from *Earth* did rise.

Honour

Honour does from *Inferiours* come :
So did the *Consuls* owe their doom,
And place, to th' *Common Votes* of *Rome.*

Her *Death* by Verfe may well be fhown ;
For *Gods* and *Goddeffes* are known
Their very Beings hence to own.

And yet this Reafon may prove lame ;
Since *Praifes,* that did *God-heads* frame,
Fall fhort when they fhould fpeak her Name.

Truth, well as *Heralds,* makes it good,
Her *Veins* fwell'd with a noble flood,
Sprung from *third Edwards* Royal blood.

Rutland an equal *Match* then brings,
Since the great *Iffue* that hence fprings,
Quarters both *Arms,* and *Blood* of *Kings.*

No pride tho did her looks attend,
Which to the lowest fhe would lend ;
As heav'nly bleffings do defcend.

Whilft fhe in that high *Orb* did move ;
She copy'd thofe bright Pow'rs above,
And gain'd both reverence and love.

Her bleffings did with luftre twine ;
Greatnefs and *Goodnefs* here did joyn
The *Sun* does fructifie, and fhine.

Her

Her *Gates,* or *Pity* never barr'd ;
Vertue, and *Innocence* her *Guard* ;
Her *Looks, obligements,* and *Reward.*

Such *Miracles* were in her fate ;
She never envy did create ;
All did admire, or imitate.

In *Youth* each noble *Lover's dream* ;
In *Age* the gaze and rule of fame ;
In *Death* the *Prieft's* and *Poet's* Theme.

How have I heard her, without noife,
Direct, and rule the publick voice ;
As each *Difcourfe* had been her choice?

How have I feen whole crouds depart,
When fhe, with her obliging Art,
Both pleas'd and captiv'd every heart.

Nor here alone was all her care ;
She left Examples, great and fair,
To caufe both wonder and defpair.

Belvoir ! thou fhalt one inftance be,
Where we the Arts of times paft fee,
Of thefe, and of Pofterity,

New builders here fhe did oppofe ;
And greater fame in this fhe chofe ;
Since here this *Frame* from ruines rofe.

Let

Let none reflect it as a fhame;
To win a good one, is lefs fame,
Than to recover a bad *Game.*

As fome *Philofophers* maintain,
'Twas lefs at firft to make a man,
Than dead, to raife him up again.

Firft fhe all fitted, and then reer'd;
Nor *David* nor his *Son* thus dar'd;
For this but us'd what that prepar'd.

So goodly and fo ftrong it fhows,
As *Mars* this ftately Caftle chofe
For his lov'd *Goddeffes* repofe.

Who views its *Beauties* and its *Power,*
At once may think of *Cæfar's Tower,*
And *Rofamund* her lovely *Bower.*

Large as her *Mind,* high as her *Fame,*
As tho fhe rais'd this *ftately Frame,*
For all that from her *Marriage* came.

And fuch a *Number* from it paft;
As have *feven* noble *Houfes* grac'd:
Here her vaft Debts are paid at laft.

For as from many a Noble Strain,
Her *Anceftors* lent to each vein;
She here repaid it all again.

What's

What's more to do then, but away,
When all is done for which we stay ?
'Tis the last *Act* commends the *Play.*

This noble *Lady* clos'd her dayes,
(After such Acts as challenge praise)
Upon that *Scene,* her self did raise.

Rare thus in life, and death, we prize
The *Phœnix* ; who with closing Eyes,
Mounts on her *Spicy Pile,* and dyes.

Her Epitaph.

Here *Braß* and *Marble* are but vainly spent ;
Her *Name,* to them, will be a *Monument.*
A lasting Fame *Posterity* must give,
Whilst *Belvoir, Mountague,* and *Rutland* live.

The C O P Y. 1676.

To the right Honourable, the Lady Anne Howe, *sixth Daughter to the Countess ; with the preceding Elegy.*

IF to pay Vows, be only due
To Persons, who can equal you ;
Then your adorers must be few.

For when in *Desarts Kings* remain,
Their *Name* and Office both are vain ;
Whilst they have none o're whom to reign.

And

And *Fame* (which is the great ones choice)
Is rais'd but by the publick noise ;
An *Eccho* from the *Peoples* voice.

Hence then my comfort is compleat ;
And my design (tho boldly great)
Has no suspition of defeat.

I often hear our *Prophets* say,
That poorest Mortals safely may,
To Heav'n, their true devotions pay.

Incourag'd thus is my design ;
The object of my tnoughts divine ;
Which here I offer at your Shrine.

When that bright *Soul* to Heav'n flew ;
Her glorious *Mantle* fell your due ;
Her Spirit doubly shar'd to You.

Your *Youth* she did so justly frame,
Both to her goodness and her fame ;
Y' are not the *Copy*, but the *same.*

She gave this *Age* a happy doom,
When she form'd you within her *Wombe* ;
And yours must bless the Age to come.

The CONSERVES. 1676.

Upon the same.

To the right honourable Mrs. Chaworth, *her Grand-Child, by Lady* Grace *Viscountess* Chaworth, *second Daughter to the Countess.*

WHEN *Angels* did on Earth appear,
 The glitt'ring Strangers treated were.
Which they vouchsaf'd only to shew
Poor Mortals what they ought to do.
They graciously made their resorts
To *Threshing-floors*, as well as *Courts*.
Where're these shining *Guests* appear'd,
Immediately were *Altars* rear'd.
On which at once their thanks they pay'd,
And for a second blessing pray'd.

Madam, there may be well suppos'd
Some curious *Confects* here inclos'd.
And bolder Poets dare reherse,
No *Conserves* like to those of *Verse*.
But nothing here deserves that name,
Unless 'tis borrow'd from my *Theme*.
And that affords such glorious prize,
It may claim favour from your *Eyes*.
Impute not, Madam, this to pride ;
You, and my *Theme* are near ally'd ;
As near as those rich *Gardens* were
To th' *Golden* Apples they did bear.

The

The PLUNDER. 1677.

To the honourable William Byron, *begging Verses*
he pleas'd to write upon my Tragedy
of Henry *the fourth.*

I'M told (and therefore well may hope for *Bayes*)
    You have been pleas'd my *Tragedy* to praise.
It unregarded was by me before,
Like a rude lump of undigested Oare.
Made current by your praise, It now may pass :
So *Princes* Stamps put value upon *Brass*.
But then your *Warrant* must be sign'd and shown ;
Else may the value of it be unknown.
The World's applause will then obedience be
To you, and your respects applause to me.
Being honour'd with your *Badge* 't will be allow'd ;
And pass, if not alone, yet in the *Crowd*.
I, all its Wit, and Worth must duly own
As yours, and by your *Mark* 'twill best be known.
For *Wit*, as your *Propriety*, is meant ;
And such Acknowledgments as this, your R*ent*.
The *Criticks* then must hazard loss and shame,
If they *distresses* make upon your claim.
Bald *Gybes*, and *Censures* hurt not so my Muse,
As they your Representatives abuse.
Bold *Grillon* and the generous *Navarre*,
I here acknowledge but your *Transcripts* are.
Your *Conversation* does the *Poet* make ;
And from your Words and Acts I *Heroes* take.

Each

Each vifit's *plunder* ; for I fteal away
More Wit at once, than would make up a *Play*.

The Badge of Good-fellowfhip.   1677.

Upon Scarlet-Faces, Rofie-Cheeks, and Ruby-Nofes.
To. C. Cooper, *Efq.*

KInd *Bacchus* does requitals fend
    For all that we *Good-fellows* fpend ;
No *Merchants* in their *Indian* trade,
Richer returns than we have made :
Tho *Pearls* for *Beads* of *Glafs* are fold,
And *Iron* purchafe fineft *Gold*.
True ! we fpend *Mony* ; where's the lofs?
All *Coin* is but authentick drofs.
The *Stamp* prefers it, and bafe need
Does all its eftimation breed.
How many years are vainly fpent,
Riches to get, and lofe content ?
In gaining it, the Day's loft quite;
And in preferving it, the Night.
    Judge now what profit may be made
Out of the jolly-drinking trade.
What tho the *Purfe* its trafh has loft ?
The *Nofe* with *Rubies* is imboft,
For *blood* that fuch rich *Bubbles* fwells,
Is *Kernel* to thofe *fhining fhells*,
Whofe luftre takes a deeper dye,
As the *good-fellow* drinks more high.
And yet the *Rubies* are but pale,
Whofe bafe extraction is from *Ale*.

How

How can the *Liver* brew what's good,
(That *Mash-fat* of the boiling blood)
When dregs of *Ale* pollute the Veins ?
As th' blood were tapt off from the *Grains*,
But when we thofe rich *Rubies* make,
With drinking *Claret, Tent,* or *Sack* ;
They take their bignefs, colour, fhape,
Fro' th' *Clufters* of the *Scarlet Grape.*
Good-fellows hence, by drinking get
That boafted thing call'd *Chimick-heat.*
Which, from the *Body,* forces out
The blood to th' *Nofe* (the *Limbeck-fpout*)
Thofe drops condens'd by the cold Air,
Advance to Rubies, and fix there.
The *Rocks* that are in *Ormus* found,
Only in pretious *Gemms* abound ;
But barren on their tops appear.
As if their heart-bloods wafted were ;
And blood of *Rocks* thofe *Rubies* are.
He who for *Tyrian-purple* feeks,
May find it in *Good-fellows* Cheeks.
The grain of *Sarra*'s only there ;
And *Bow-dies* firft invented were
From fome old *Brewer,* who liv'd there.
Canary fo refines the Skin,
The blood's tranfparent from within.
That modeft blufh which *Virgins* boaft,
Had long fince from the *World* been loft ;
But for *ftrong-liquor* and a *Toaft.*
Nay,-which is more--**Phyficians** prove,
That -- *Sanguin temper* which all love,

Soma

Some *Red-nos'd Drinker* rais'd the Breed,
Transfusing't to his happy Seed.

 Sack makes not only *ruby'd Noses,*
But in our *Cheeks* plants *Beds of Roses:*
For as the heav'nly dew, first drops
Upon the Rose-Trees pregnant tops;
Feeding them with prolifick blood,
Untill they *belly* to a *Bud :*
Phœbus his *Midwifry* then shows,
And in green *Mantles* layes the *Rose.*
The *Juice* so of the lusty *Grape,*
On *Madam Temperance* acts a *Rape ;*
Swelling our *Cheeks* with seeds of *Roses,*
Which *Bacchus's* heat to th' World discloses ;
In those hot *Beds* they'l freshly last,
In spite of Frost, or Winters blast.

 Then let *Red-Noses* henceforth be
No subjects for vain *Drollery.*
'Tis sawey here our Wits to try ;
Scarlet's the *badge* of *Majesty.*
Kings buy their pomp; when *Drinkers* have
Their *Shop,* and in themselves are brave.
Roses in *June* are only blown ?
Good-Fellows theirs all th' year are shown.
A *Virgins blush* is rul'd by th' *Moon ;*
Their *Tides* soon flow, and ebb as soon :
When as *Good-Fellows* never shrink
Till *Death;* that is, till they want drink.
Its virtues are not half told yet ;
It heightens *Valour,* quickens *wit ;*
The *Heart* is cheerd, *Friendship* increast;
No care, but for some harmless *Jest.*

Then

POEMS

POEMS. 173

Then let's not leave it, tho some scold,
Because *phanatical*, or *old*:
Let such grave *Fops* inslave their will
He who made these, will drink on still.

The R E N T. 1677.
To the Honourable Lady, Mrs. Chaworth.

O'R worn with cares, and ag'd with discontent;
I'm scarcely able to procure your *Rent*.
Tho *Poverty*, and *Poetry* may hit;
Tenants, I'm sure, it will but odly fit.
Besides a double Obligation's due;
Since I have paid most Persons off, but you.
No greater happiness could me befall ;
Not that I'm quit from them, but owe you all.
Poor Debtors so (that are behind hand hurl'd,
Frown'd on above by'th *Stars*, below by th' *World*,)
Contract their *Mortgages*; One mortal wound
Less pain, than living to be flead, is found.
One *Massy Fetter* (tho its weight be more)
Is far less troublesome than half a score:
None (tho with *Bracelets*) would be hung all o're.
A *Dungeon's* easier, than at once to be
Both *Stockt*, and *Whipt*, and on the *Pillory*.
Thus roving *Lovers* that diffuse their Fires,
(New objects always kindling fresh desires)
Catching the flame, like *Powder*, at a touch,
Ne'r rightly love, because they love too much :
So men in Debt almost to every one,
Are so distracted, they can pay to none.

Mv

My several lines of Obligations due
To others, now concenter all in you.
But, *Madam,* as each *Debt* to *Heav'n* requires
The *Stock* o'th' *Heart,* and *use* of our *Desires* ;
So mine shall be as justly paid to you;
Both in the *Principal,* and *Int'rest* too.

The NEW-YEAR'S GIFT.

To the same. 1677.

MY *Rent* is paid ; but something is behind ;
There I was just, but here I must be kind.
Th' expression suits with voluntary things ;
And such are *Presents* , altho made to *Kings,*
'Tis true they honour us, when they receive,
But still it shows a kindness when we give.
Of all your *New-year's-gifts* mine is the least ;
Yet none gives better, than who gives his best.
As I were studying what this *best* might be ;
Intranc'd I fell into an *Extasie.*
I 'spi'd i'th' Airy *Region,* from a far,
A shining thing shoot like a *falling Star*
As it drew nearer my astonisht sight,
Still did it bigger seem, and still more bright.
So dazling fierce its neighb'ring glories grew ;
Mine Eyes I hid, unable for the view.
Wip'd thrice with some soft thing,   I was so bold
To look what't were ; and found it *downy* Gold :
The lining of the *Wing* of my *bright Guest*
A young and glitt'ring *form,* all heav'nly drest.

Fear

Fear not, it said ; I've laid my *lightning* by,
It else would melt the *Chryſtal* of thine *Eye*,
And work effects ſo contrary-- Its light
Would cloud thy ſickning beams with laſting night.
Hail *off-ſpring* of the Morning, I did cry *!*
Or art thou not *Aurora's* ſelf, ſaid I ?
Or ſome *Angelic-form*, that hath put on
The *Veil* of that fair *Sex* ? Know I am none
Of all thy flatt'ring gheſſes, then it ſaid ;
Yet, tho ſo bright, I'm but to them a ſhade.
One that attends upon the *Theſpian Quires* ⎫
Deſign'd to warm thy breaſt with nobler fires ; ⎬
To rule thy *Fancy*, heighten thy *Deſires*. ⎭
The *Heav'nly-Muſe* I am, whom thou doſt wrong,
Imploying me in every idle *Song*.
I was forſaking thee ; and now would go ;
But for the *Lady* thou art writing to.
To *her* I'le from the *Muſes's* ſervice run : ⎫
By her thoſe *ſhining Ladies* are out-ſhone ; ⎬
And yet they are *Daughters of the Sun*. ⎭
A *New-years-gift* thou want'ſt. Let me be it ,
Or I'll condemn thee to the dearth of Wit.
Seis'd ſhall thine Humour and thy Fancy be
As forfeited ; for both belong to me :
But if thou wilt me with her ſervice grace, ⎫
Henceforth imploying me to ſing her praiſe, ⎬
I'll from *Apollo's Daphne* get the *Bayes*. ⎭
No with'ring *Springs*, but ſuch as ſhall have root ;
Whoſe *living wreaths* about thy *brows* ſhall ſhoot.
Thus, *Madam*, I out-doe my former uſe ;
Then I gave *Verſes*, now I give my *Muſe*.

The VIRGIN. 1677.

Epitaph upon my dear S. Mrs. S. S.

IF *Duſt* imbalm'd inricht the Soyl,
　Making ſuch *Tombs* intice to ſpoil ;
She needs muſt yield a richer prize,
Imbalm'd with Virtue more than Spice.
This Stone ſhe turns into a *Shrine,*
Making the *Grave* become a *Mine.*
Her precious worth, like *Ingotts,* ſhines,
And is new *minted* in theſe Lines.

Read, if thou canſt, with unwet eyes,
Where *Vertues Darling* bury'd lies.
Fair as the Sun ; yet ſcorn'd to twiſt
Her *Virgin Splendor* with a *Miſt* ;
Chaſter than *Snow,* unmelted tryes
The hotteſt beames of amorous eyes.
Her *Looks,* at *Sin* and *Luſt* incens'd,
Like *Cherubim* her *Eden* fenc'd.

Yet if the World can imitate
Her Vertues, tis a happier fate
Than if ſhe had left Children here.
Theſe *mortal,* thoſe *immortal* are.

CREDE

P O E M S. 177

CREDE BYRON. 1677.

To the Honourable William Byron, *upon a Paper of Verses sent me -- upon a Present to the most beautiful Ladies his Daughters.*

These are the Verses.

YOU, like the gen'rous Sun, do still dispence,
    To those that merit least, your influence.
Your *Obligations* have that pow'rful charm ;
They need must conquer, when they first disarm.
The *Favours,* you so freely have bestow'd,
Are such we ne'r deserv'd, nor you e're ow'd.
The *Debt* is mine I own ; I ought to pay ;
But, like a *Bankrupt,* beg a longer Day :
They're brisk, and young ; and can another way.
My *Muse* I should excuse, she's dull and rude;
Those that do write to you in Verse intrude;
Were not her *Products* all from Gratitude.
Presumption is a crime, but worse *despair* ;
One errs in boldness, and the other fear.
But I presume you'l pardon the first Fault :
The Man's a *Coward* that ne'r makes Assault.
In such *Atchievements* if I chance to dye ;
I live in fame, if in your memory.
My whole ambition only does extend
To gain the name of *Shipman*'s faithful Friend.
And tho I cannot amply speak your praise ;
I'le wear the *Myrtle,* tho you wear the *Bayes.*

W. B.

N   *In*

In return to these.

DID not Heav'ns blessings rich requitals bring,
Constant Devotion were a tiresome thing.
Our int'rest 'tis tho , thus to spend our *Dayes*,
Blessings to pray for, and when gain'd, to praise.
In this blest *Circle* you and I do move ;
Your Love my Duty gains, and that your Love.
My Gratitude owns all you gave before,
And is an *Earnest* here to purchase more.
Yet when, on grateful *Altars*, *Incense* burns,
The Virtue's lost, if we expect returns ;
And looks as *Subjects* should with *Princes* vye,
Exacting honour for their *Loyalty*.
But I'll with reverence wait, and faithful be ;
Be *noble Byron* what he will to me.
Your Favours lose no virtue by delay ;
You grant me those for which I dare not pray :
Oh, teach the *Ladies*, Sir, your *winning* way.
To be your *Friend* is such a glorious name,
It urges merit, and it offers fame :
I, from the *Commons*, rise your *Buckingham*.
This heightens me above the common view,
And makes me thus expostulate with you.
    Was't not enough your *Ancestors* did aid
The *mighty Norman*, when he did invade ?
Whose *noble Acts* increast their former store,
And here confirm'd those *Honours* they brought o're
Is't not enough that this *Illustrious Line*
Succeeds in you, and you maintain the *Shine* ?
Differing but thus fro'th' glory they have won,
They were the *Morning*, you the *Mid-day Sun* ?

Is't

Is't not enough the *Byrons* all excell,
As much in loving, as in fighting well?
Witness their *Motto*, prov'd in *Bosworth* Field,
Where *Truth* did their triumphant *Chariot* gild.
Is not that fame enough your *Noble Sire*,
With his *six noble Brothers*, did acquire?
All valiant *Knights*! whose *Title* was not bought,
But under *Charls* his *Royal standard* sought.
Is't not enough that *Brittish Coronet*
Circles your head, your *Ancestors* did get?
But you must thirst after inferiour praise,
And from the *Brittish Bards* too gain the *Bayes*?
The *Civic-Garland* and the *Mural* too,
Are by succession your unquestion'd due.
The *Lawrel Crown* you may by title claim;
Honour's reward is *Tribute* to your *Name*.
But this of *Bayes* your humour may condemn,
Be not our *Rival* since you are our *Theme*.
Nobler Acquists than these, you have design'd;
Honour and *Glory* must inflame your *Mind*.
Your *Inroads* only into *Verse* are made,
Like mighty *Monarchs* that *small States* invade.
It is not worth their while: the chiefest charms
Are to get fame and terrour by their *Arms*.
To big you are in *Verse* to be confin'd
Verse is too narrow for your *worth*, or *Mind*

But I am impudent, nay worse, profane,
To make your courtship of the *Muses* vain:
As tho there were disparagement i'th' thing;
When I would gladly do't were I a *King*.
Upon two *Poles* the *Soul* (like *Heav'n*) does move,
The bright and lasting *Poles* of *Wit*, and *Love*.

N 2

Nor

Nor *Wit*, nor *Love*, of *Rivals* will admit ;
We jealous are in *Love*, but more in *Wit*.
But I offend more in this vain excuse ;
Since you already have injoy'd the *Muse*.
She's yours by mutual choice ; then 'tis not fit,
That her good *Graces* I should seek to get ;
For that would be th' *Adultery* of *Wit*.
Sometimes you entertain her for your Sport;
So th' *Players* have admittance to the *Court*.
The *Roman Consul* with his *Children* play'd ;
And *Jove* Sports sometimes with his *Ganimede*.
After such *Toying* she'l inconstant be ;
And your attraits will make her *cuckold* me.

T. S.

W I T and N A T U R E. 1677.

A Pindaric Ode to Sr. Edw. Rich.

GReat *Nature*, hail!
 Who over mankind do'st prevail.
Queen Regent of this sublunary *Frame*,
 Distinguish't by what ever **Name**,
For *Metaphysick Notions* I lay by,
 Thin subtleties for me too high.
 Such *Thee* define
 To be the *Art* Divine,
 Or the eternal *fixt decree*,
From all inferiour appealments free ;
The fil'd *Record* in *Heaven*'s high *Chancery*:
 This is methinks an over-rate
 Or they confound thy State ;
Not well distinguishing 'twixt *thee* and *Fate*.

Such

Such myſtick definitions puzzle more,
    Blinding Eyes but dim before.
Whoſe ſtudies, like your *Oxford's*, ſeem to be
    The *Magick* of *Divinity.*

      Be what it will,
    In me- It ſhews its magick skill.
Its pow'rful charms to *Poetry* inclin'd
      My youthful mind.
    Caſtalian Liquor did imbue
     My *Veſſel* whilſt 't were new.
No other reliſh it will own.
Each drop that from the *Dregs* is ſpilt,
    (For now I am o' th' *Tilt*)
Has ſome ſmall taſte of *Helicon.*
Nor herein will I *Nature* blame ;
Let great and rich-Men buſtle for a name ;
    We, we muſt raiſe their fame.
    That's more for ours, than their Renown,
'Tis a *Regalio* of *Apollo's Crown,*
    From him all beams of *Glory* flow ;
Heroes are mighty things indeed but *Poets* make 'em ſo.

    From this imperial height to which I'm flown
      I tumble down.
Give me a *Cypreſs* not a *Lawrel Crown* !
     With deteſtation, I eſpy
    The *Scandals* upon *Poetry.*
Shall burning *Luſt* be ſaid or heating *Wine,*
    The breaſts of *Poets* to refine ;
     Is the *Bay* more freſhly leav'd,
    When with the *Vine* 'tis interweav'd ?
       N 3   *Coy*

Coy Daphne, ſilence break;
Let thy *Rind* chap into a *Mouth*, and ſpeak.
Would not *Apollo*'s Rape more grateful be
Than *Bacchus Love*, tho he ſhould marry thee?
Can we produce no happy thought,
Unleſs betwixt a *Muſe* and *Satyr* got?
Have thoſe chaſt *Virgins* chang'd their loves,
And left *Pierian Groves*,
To ramble up and down,
And be like *Miſſes* of thè *Town*?
Say whether fate is more renown'd
To be à *Dutcheſs* crown'd;
Or with *immortal Glories* ſhining round?

Nature —— I cannot yet define;
More fit for ſome *Seraphical Divine*:
Tho they but *Graces* three, and we have *Muſes* nine.
To wreaths of *Bay* they have ſufficient claim,
Their *Sions* holy Hill
Out-rivals our *Parnaſſus* in its fame.
And *Hermon*'s ſacred *Dew*
Will give an Influence as true
As *Aganippe* s Rill.
Prieſts we are both alike, and both alike are fir'd
With ſacred heat: *Poets* have been inſpir'd,
Shar'd in their gifts of *Prophecy*,
As they in ours of *Poetry*,
And both have *Lawrels* won;
They have their *Doctor Sprat*, & had their *Doctor Donne*

Nor do we come behind.
The *Muſes*, and the *Graces* too
Have *Lay-men* courted oft, and yet they do,
And ſome of us too are to them inclin'd. *Davi*

David the golden Age did gild;
His *Harp*, as lasting glory as his *Swond* did yield;
And he intit'led to as fair renown,
  By *Wreaths* of *Bay*, as *Judah's Crown.*
Virgil the *Silver Age* did cause to shine.
The *Iron Age Cleveland* and *Cowley* had ;
  Both of them, alas, are dead
And with em too, I fear, their heat divine!
  But stay! some comfort yet does come,
We have good *Poets* store, as-- faith I know not whom ;
But this *Pindarick* rapture has convey'd
  Me from my first intent,
  I had some faint *Ideas* made,
  How I might Nature represent.
To her I would a glorious *Substance* give,
  Compos'd of *Body* and of *Soul.*
She does a mighty *Sovereign* live,
  Ruling from this, to th' other *Pole.*
What is her *Body, Muse,* then say ?
  'Tis *Beauty,* that bright *Ray* ;
The *Copy* of a *Summers* shining *Day,*
  Just when *Aurora* meets the *Sun.*
And yet the fair *Original* by th' *Copy* is out-done.

  When She's so drest
  She's fine,
 As when a glittering Vest
Adorns an *Angel* ; when the *Silver Light*
Peeps through the *azure Tinsel,* that does line
The *shining Robe,* and makes it heav'nly bright.
  Her rosie blushes shine
  Quite through the *Lilly skin* :

As *shooting Flame* through *burnt White-Wine*:
The outward *Stuff*'s so thin,
The *Scarlet lining* all appears within.
Her bright and piercing eye
Can by no *Clouds* be hid;
But quite shines through the *Lid*:
As *Sun-beams* thorough *Chrystal* fly.
Nay, hers excell; their light does stay,
And knows no *West*, no *setting Sun* ;
Here's almost everlasting *day*,
As at the *Poles*, where *Night* is seldome known

If we such rare attractions owe
To *Nature's Body*; then (without controul)
We must far greater know,
When we're acquainted with her *Soul*.
Then, *Muse*, 'tis very fit,
Thou tell'st us it.
It is that pow'rful pleasant thing call'd *Wit*.
Wit is the *Soul* of *Nature*! but what more
In troth I cannot tell.
But I will shew where it does dwell;
And you can ask no more.
Some starve it out; and so unfortunate am **I**!
Some starve it too with *Luxury* ;
Some seek to murder it in *Rhyme* ;
And some with *Clinches* torture it to death;
Some others guilty of the *Hangman*'s crime,
With *strong Lines* stop its breath.
Then sometimes it does stay
With those who plenty know ;
But they soon weary grow,

An

POEMS. 185

And it is turn'd away,
On all accounts as well content as they.
It sometimes for its habitation payes,
As when our *Poets Mony* get for *Plaies*;
Before 'twas never heard
That they did seek reward,
Unless it was a Crown of *Bayes*.
For if *Mecænas* would some favours give;
They, in requital made *Mecænas* live.
But great ones are our *Rivals* grown
In these ill-humour'd days,
As though they had suspition,
To live in no *Verse* but their own;
Like *Nero*, now they *fiddle* too for praise.

But where's this place of *Wit*?
For I before did promise it.
After the strict re-searches I have made,
I fear'd that it above was fled,
After *Astræa*, that fair heav'nly *Maid*.
Till *Friday* last I gain'd a view;
And after much cold *hunting* too;
I did recover my last *Game*, and found it, Sir, in you.

The ANTIQUARY. 1677.

Upon the Baronage of England, *by Sr.* Will. Dugdale,
Garter-Principal King at Arms.

A Selden, or a *Camden*'s only fit
To judge, and praise the *Works* that he has writ.
So noble *structures*, by rare Artists rais'd,
Should only by *Vitruvius* rules be prais'd,

Praise

Praise is a *Tax* by *Justice*-self thought fit ;
And every worthy man has claim to it.
Which should as strictly be to *merit* paid,
As *Taxes* that by *Parliaments* are made.
Authentick praises should these *Works* regard,
Such as at once bring *Honour* and *Reward.*
Prodigious were the pains that brought them forth ;
By nothing to be equal'd, but their worth.
Here *England's* rising splendors he has shown,
Till come to Man-hood in its glorious Noon ;
-----But now alas !-----
Small are the shadows of its Evening Sun.
Her *honours* streams he from the *Fountain* brings,
Guiding the *Current* to the lower Springs.
Obstructions in each *Channel* he does clear ;
As if the *Law of Sewers* govern'd here.
His active knowledge has the searching force
Of Spirits, that can see, and not discourse.
Strange penetrating art ! to pierce, like *Air,*
Each close recess, and ransack all things there.
Rare Learning that reveals as clear as Light,
The secret Treasures both of *Time* and *Night.*
Which like the Sun throughout the World can pry,
And is at once to't self both *Light* and *Eye.*
In *Graves* (those shades of *Death*) now *Life* is found,
As quickning heat brings *Flowers* from the Ground.
No *Marble* Tombs, no *Pyramids* can hold
From turning like the *Dust* they did infold.
Names, tho long lost in *Rubbish,* own his power :
As *Chymists* can from *Ashes* raise a *Flower.*
Of *Statues* long defac'd, and smooth as *Glass,*
As in a *Chrystal,* here he shews the *Face.*

If

If any part be left, he can it own :
Hercules here may by his *Foot* be known.
From ftragling characters in worn-out *Deeds*,
Th' intrigues of ancient *Families* he reads.
Succeffions vary'd to and fro agen,
(*Alcides*-like) he traces to their D*en*.
Thofe *Families* that loft themfelves, and run
Into a various fucceffion ;
He does reduce to their firft *Marriage*-Bed ;
And fhews *fev n-chanel'd Nile* its *Fountain* Head.
  For all this coft, but Mortal aid he brings,
As all muft do, that write of mortal things.
Tho his efforts are of the ftrongeft rate,
Yet cannot fave what is condemn'd by Fate.
Stones thus, that crown a lofty *Turret's* head,
May pave the Ground for ev'ry foot to tread.
Marbles muft moulder, *Steel* confume with Ruft ;
Crowns, with their *Owners*, all refolve to *Duft*.
Nor there fecure ! that very *Duft* be gone,
Into the vaft *Abyfs* of *Air* be blown ;
The fport of *Winds*, who kept the *World* in fear ;
Their *Duft* as reftlefs as their thoughts were here.

R E D   C A N A R Y.   1677.

With fome Bottles of it----To the right honourable
Katharine *Lady* Roos, *&c.*

TH' infpired few, whofe glowing breafts
    Refin'd 'em for *Apollo's* Priefts ;
When myftick heat their bloods did fire,
Themfelves did from themfelves retire.

Banifht

Banisht the *mortal* from their breast,
That *Presence-Chamber* richly drest ;
The glorious *Furniture* all thin'd ;
For with *Apollo's* self 'twas lin'd.
What charming words might needs fume hence.
Mixt with that neigh'bring Influence,
Whose thickning breath appear'd to be
A *Chariot* for the *Deity.*
   Were my *Productions* but so blest.
Your Ladiship might be exprest.
But Poetsnow heed no such fires ;
Yet still some *Deity* inspires.
Venus or *Bacchus* height'ns sence,
Tho with malignant influence.
Those *Dæmons* now profane our *Groves*
With vain, or with dishonest loves ;
Making a *Desart* of the place,
With'ring the *Mirtles* and the *Bays* :
The *Fiend* thus, with contagious vice.
Blasted the *Trees* of *Paradice.*
But, Madam, your illustrious *name* ⎫
Is both my *Influence* and *Theme* ; ⎬
Refining all my *Smoak* to *flame.* ⎭
Hence baffled *Poetry* may thrive,
And *Oracles* again revive.
Its clouded beams may brighter rise, ⎫
Kindled by th' Sun-shine of your eyes, ⎬
As *Persians* fire their *Sacrifice.* ⎭
'Till th' *Muses* have that bliss obtain'd,
They're like fall'n *Stars* in darkness chain'd.
Then farewel *Poetry*!

B

— But ſtay —
Venus may prove *Urania.*
She may injoy that happy fate,
If ſhe your virtues imitate.
Her *Chariot* then, through th' *heav'nly lawn,*
By *Doves,* not *Sparrows* will be drawn :
And virtuous *Love* henceforward boaſt,
You have reſtor'd what *Venus* loſt.

But, Madam, 'tis too ſad a truth,
Bacchus is ſo debauch'd a youth ;
That *Lees* as ſoon will leave his *Wine,*
As his corruptions he'll refine.
Ill humours ſooneſt are withſtood,
And cured beſt by letting blood :
That hot-braind *God,* with fumes oppreſt,
Bleeds here ſome ounces of his beſt.
His *Heart-blood-drops* he offers here
To you his fair *Deliverer* ;
The *Stoick* ſo himſelf reſign'd,
(Hence owning the *eternal mind.*)
And thus his beſt *Drops* did prefer
To *Jove,* the great *Deliverer.*

This my *Oblation* may attone
For all offences he has done.
If in your Favour it finds place,
The *Reprobate* recovers Grace.
Your influence then muſt be divine ; ⎫
Since, Madam, it can thus refine ⎬
The dregs of *Love,* of *Wit,* of *Wine.* ⎭

The

The HUFFER. 1677.

Spoken by Ant. Eyre Esquire, *and directed to the right Honourable, the* Lady Roos, *when he acted* Alman-zor *in the* Granada, *at* Belvoir; *in way of Prologue.*

I That made *Fortune* Lacky by my side,
　Had *Fame* for *Trumpet,* and *Success* for *Guide* :
I that did conquer *Armies* with a word,
Making *Fate* yield to my more pow'rful *Sword*:
I that could with a *Smile* bestow a *Crown,*
Then blast my new rais'd *Monarch* with a *Frown.*
Almanzor, I, who (by the *Poet* taught)
Huft more, than ever *Hero* did, or ought :
I now submit, and lay my *Lawrels* down ;
But from your favours hope a nobler *Crown.*

Whence is this sudden calm? what could controul
The working passion of my boistrous *Soul?*
My breast did like some *Northern Climate* show,
Its fountain froze, and cover'd o're with *Snow.*
Thaw'd, *Ladies,* by your Eyes (those *Mid-day Suns*)
The melting *Spring* drops *Rubies,* as it runs.
My *Blood,* once safe under this *Icy Lock,*
Softens like *Coral* on the *melting Rock.*
No *Lapland Spell,* can temper any *Arms*
To be of proof,'gainst *Beauties* stronger charms.
And one amongst those *Ladies* I have 'spi'd,
Whose pointed rayes wound more than *Almahide.*

Nature, and *Dryden,* all that both could do
To perfect *Almahide,* falls short of you.

Tho

Tho they advance the luftres of her Eyes,
Above the *Stars* o' th' *Rocks*, or *Gemms* o' th' *Skies*:
When you appear, their fickly beams give way,
Like frighted *Phantoms* to the fpringing *Day*.
Nay I, who thought no paffions me could move,
Be'ng free from fear, and therefore free from Love.
Greater than *Nature*, you my *Heart* conftrain'd ;
And *Love* has now his ftubborn *Rebel chain d*:
Yet not content to reft his Empire there,
It's doubly chain'd ; and now inflav'd to fear.
Two ftrong *Difeafes* I at once indure,
Yet as an *Ague* does from *Plagues* fecure;
My trembling Fear, left I prefumptuous prove,
Allayes the raging *Peftilence* of *Love*.

The REPRESENTATION. 1677.

Upon the Honourable Mrs. Bridget Noel, *acting the*
Part of Almahide, *in* Dryden's Granada, *at* Belvoir.

AStonifh'd Mufe! now thou haft gain'd thy *Tongue*,
Exalt thy fancy in a noble *Song*.
Thy honour'd *Belvoir* (that moft pregnant *Wombe*
Of *Wonders*) with amazement ftruck thee dumb:
Thus the old doubtful *Prieft*, his *Lips* were feal'd,
When that bright Gueft i' th' *Temple* was reveal'd.
Surpriz'd alike, I filently retir'd ;
Withdrew my *Soul*, and inwardly admir'd
That fuch a Lady on the *Stage* was feen,
Lefs'ning her felf to reprefent a *Queen*.
Confcious of which, her *Cheeks* with *Scarlet* dy'd,
Show'd *Modefty* in her moft Royal pride :

Heav'n's

Heav'n's Face is fleckt fo, when the bafhful Light
Muffles her Glories in the Clouds of Night.
Miftake me not, her Splendors were not gone ;
They only feem'd fo, like the fetting Sun.
Like him, fhe in her felf is always bright,
Though not to us, plac'd in a vary'd light.
She may confirm the *Tartar Princes*'s lot,
That *Stories* fay, was by the *Sun-beams* got.
Her *Bodie*'s cloath'd with light ; the *Sky*'s her *Skin* ,
(That glorious *Curtain* of the *Heav'n* within ;)
Her circ'ling *Blood* (like to the *Worlds bright* Eye)
Rounds all her World, and glitters through her *Sky*
Dangers may come then by too near a view ;
Her beams both dazzle may, and burn us too.
For *Light* is *Fire*, altho but thinly fpread ;
Through *burning Glaffes* of her *Eyes* convey'd.

Mongft all thofe flames fh has none that inward glow,
Nor feels the heat that warms our *World* below :
Cold is her Blood, as tho with *Julips* fed ;
Not ftrange, fince in a *Snow-houfe* it is laid.
Froft in her *Blood*, tho *Fire* is in her *Eyes* :
Thus *Lightning* from the *coldeft Region* flyes.

Whilft the *Town-fcumm* (thofe *Midianites o'th Stage*)
Surprize the *Zimries* of this wifling Age ;
Apparent dangers muft to us accrue,
Since real *Princes* here may juftly woo.
Beautie's fair *Goddefs*, and the *Queen of Night*,
When gaudi'ft in their tiffu'd robes of Light,
Tread not th' Etherial *Stage* with greater ftate ;
Tho *Gods* themfelves from them attend their fate.
Whirl'd in their *Sphears* (thofe *bright Machines*) they fly
Quite through the fpace of their archt-roof of th' Sky.

Nor

Nor does the *simile* unfit appear,
Or for this *Actor*, or this *Theater*.
Formerly, when the *Prophets* zeals were fir'd,
By pow'rs which they ador'd, they were inspir'd.
Blest age ! wherein the *Oracles* of Wit
Were sacred *Dictates* from the *Altar* Writ.
When *Poets*, were the *Trumpets* that convey'd
Those formed sounds that by the Gods were made.
Then from the *Deities* they gain'd respect ;
But now from heedless *Mortals* find neglect :
Immortal Verse sprung from immortal aids ;
Now *Misses* rule, then rul'd the *Thespian Maids*.
Hence they of future things divinely writ ;
Now past and present fooleries are Wit ;
Poems, and *Poets*, one another fit.

It must be so, now thirst of *Fame*'s away, (the *Bay*:
Quencht with large *Draughts*, and th'*Vine* out-grows
Whilst *Farces* and such *Vices* of the *Stage*,
Corrupt the *Poetry* of this loose Age.
No *Heroe*, no *Mecænas* in these times,
For *Subject*, or *incouragement* of *Rhymes*.
Dryden alone, has got some Title now
To th' *Lawrel* wreaths, that grace his lucky *Brow*.
Tho neither *Deity* nor *Muse* inspires,
Her breath alone fann'd his Poetick fires.
Th' old custom is to his advantage broke ;
For here he made those words the Goddess spoke.
Blest by her Mouth, they may obtain the fate
Of Oracles, and gain as long a date.
Thus his rude *Oare* cast in that precious *Mould*,
Lost all its *Dross*, and turn'd *refined Gold*.

She did create its worth, and *made* the *Play*;
And breath'd the *breath* of *Life* into *his Clay.*

The VISION. 1677.

To the Right Honourable the Lady Roos, *&c.* Upon
the Birth of the Heir of Rutland.

THis *Night* injoys fo fweet a calm;
   As th *Air* diffolv'd it felf to *Balm.*
So deep a *filence* all things keep,
As *Nature's* felf were hufh't afleep.
Cynthia neglects her watch i'th' Skies,
And drowzy too has clos'd her eyes.
Or is with her *Endymion,* hid
Under fome cloudy *Coverlid.*
Yet light I through her *Curtains* 'fpy,
Scap'd from the corner of her Eye.

But foon the *Harbinger* of *Day*
Chas'd all thofe *gloomy fhades* away:
With *Rofes* ftrew'd the *Paths* o'th' *Eaft,*
Till *Tethys* had her *Lover* dreft.
That way I turn'd my ready eye;
When I your *Belvoir* did efpy
(For all our *Vale* is fully *Weft,*
And *Belvoir* is its Sun i'th' *Eaft*)
I gaz'd---the other *Sun* to 'fpy;
When thence a thing did fwiftly'r fly
   ——— than *Light*
Which in one moment gilds the *Sky.*
Gently to me the *Vifion* came,
Snatching me up with arms of flame:

And me through yielding Air convey'd,
In *Belvoir* Chappel fafely laid.

The facred *Genii* of the place,
Whence it both fafety takes, and grace;
Bright *Off-fprings* of cœleftial race.
Their downy *Pinnions-Gold* out-vy'd,
All o're with fparkling *Diamonds* ey'd.
Flying about the facred *Frame*,
They fann'd the ambient Air to flame;
Or from their eyes the *lightning* came.
After fome *Ceremonies* paft;
They fung ———
———' Our *Belvoir* now fhall laft :
'Our *Habitations* are fecure ;
' The Honour of our *Charge* is fure.
Flying about, ftrange *Mufick* plaid ;
Their founding *Wings* a *Confort* made,
As every fhining *Quill* therein,
A well-tun'd *Organ-pipe* had been.

Amaz'd (as well I might) I fpoke;
And up the *Conventicle* broke.
All vanifht but my flaming *Guide* ;
Who to my wond'ring thoughts reply'd.
' This night thou art a *Prophet* crown'd ;
' For *Belvoir* now an *Heir* has found.
'The blufhing *Portals* of its *Eaft*
' Are with an infant *Phœbus* bleft.
'With *native fcarlet* he was born :
' As *Rofes* cloath the *Chryfome Morn*.

" This ancient *Earldom* boaſt now may,
" Its honour finds a full-grown *Day*
" *Great Rutland is* the *Evening bright*, ⎤
" Safe guarded from approaching *Night* ; ⎬
" His own *ſeven Stars* preſerve his light. ⎦
" *Illuſtrious Roos*, that *full-ripe Sun*—
" Supplies the glorious place of *Noon* ;
" All ſhining in *Meridian* beams :
" Like *Virtue* crown'd 'twixt two extreams.
" That *Infant of the Sun*, new born,
" *Rutland i' th' Cradle, Sol i' th' Morn* ;
" Iucirc'led with a gentle blaze
" Reflected from his Mothers Face ;
" 'Till her clos'd Eyes have made the Night,
" Amaz'd ours cannot bear her light.
" This makes us at this *Seaſon* play,
" Like *Birds* of *Night*, avoiding *Day*.
" W'are tho the *Genii* of this *Place*,
" Attendants of this noble Race.
" Thy ready *Zeal* wee'l ſo inflame,
" By offring, thou ſhalt purchaſe fame.
" Thy *Incenſe* from the *Vale* ſhall riſe,
" And crown with curled Clouds theſe Skies,
" Untill their *Jove* his *golden ſhow'rs*
" Upon thy barren *Danae* pours.
" Thought I this *Angel* may ſay true ;
" Elſe he is in a *Viſion* too.

You, Madam, prove ſo rich a *Theme*,
You can make *Poets* in a *Dream*.

The

The MUSICIAN. 1677.

Upon the Death of Mr. W. D. excellent in Musick,
Servant at Belvoir.

OF those *five Senses* that our *Nature* grace,
Seeing, and *Hearing*, have the noblest place.
By th' *Eares*, the Soul its chiefest bliss obtains;
And showes by th' *Eyes* those blessings that it gains.
Those others to the *Body* more belong,
And th' *heav'nly Guest* oft by excesses wrong.
Whose grosser humours we can serve at home,
But must to *Belvoir* for the purer come.
What choicer Object can indear the *Sight*?
Above the Earth as much in worth, as height.
A *second Eden* shining all about;
Glorious within, and beautiful without!

Then for to please the *Ears* (those *Doors* o'th' *Mind*)
Where could we rarer choice of treatments find?
What wonders have I from his *Musick* known?
Passions to raise in all breasts but his own.
His *Viol* more than *Magick Spells* could do,
Both raise our *Tempests*, and then calm 'em too,
Each *Finger* was a *Tongue*, and could impart
Persuasive force, above *Rhetorick* art.
The Stubborn Passions he might well command,
When every Heart was in his pow'ful hand.
Here a soft charming Air for Mast'ry tries,
With *Venus* breath, and mov'd more than her Sighs.
There from his *Bow* darts forth a piercing strain,
Wounds more than *Cupid*, and yet brings no pain.

When

When he his fpeaking *Violin* laid by,
And would his *Fl agelt* or *Cornet* try ;
The wanton Air he'd in chafte meafures bind,
To gentle founds tuning th' unruly Wind.
Strada's fam'd *Lutænift* his art might fail,
And dye for fhame before this *Nightingale.*
Whofe peaceful Soul did for its change prepare,
And vanifht calmly in a well-tun'd Air.
But all mifchances here are fo ingroft ;
Not th' *Artift* only, but the *Art* is loft.
Thus their fad fate the *Græcians* did lament ;
Their *Orpheus,* and his *Harp* together went.

To my refpected Friend, Capt. Shipman. 1678.

TO you, as to my *Guardian,* I go ;
 To ask protection from a mighty *Foe.*
My tender *Mufe,* frighted with *Critick's* fame,
Starts, and gives back, when fhe but hears the name.
She's young, and dares not hope to come to good ;
Yet ftrangely dreads a blighting in the bud.
So little Birds, below the *Fowler's* care,
Moft apprehend the danger of the fnare.
And whilft he fhoots at fome more noble prize,
They hear the ecchoing noife, and trembling rife.

It is prefumption in my worthlefs *Mufe*
To ask your help, worthy a better ufe.
Yet fhe's ambitious, and defires to live ;
And fays, if you'l vouchfafe your *Pafs* to give ;
She's fure no *Critick* dares againft you ftrive.

When

When I confider how the mighty *Jove*
Receiv'd the Token of the poor *Bee*'s love;
Methinks I cann't but hope-- that as a *Friend*
You'l not defpife (I'm fure you cann't commend)
That wᶜʰ fcarce half an hour both thought & penn'd.

SPRING and AUTUMN. 1678.
To that hopeful Gentleman, Jo. Howe, *Efq; In anfwer*
to the fore-going Verfes.

THe fruitful *Trees*,that fhade the Southern Climes,
Are like the *blooming* fancies in your Rhymes.
Where *Spring*, and *Autumn*, in one feafon meet,
The fruit delicious, and the bloffoms fweet.
You need no Guardian, but *Apollo*'s care ;
And that which makes you bud,will make you bear.
Fruits,with fuch early *Sun-fhine* grac'd, muft grow,
And bear, and flourifh, and no blaftings know.
Secure from *Criticks*--their fharp frofty Air
Serves but to nip your *Lady-Mufe* more fair.
Their *Ginns*, and *Cenfures* are but needlefs found:
Snares ufelefs are for *Birds* that fcorn the ground.

Your youthful *Mufe* deferves the choiceft note:
So *Effences* are from *firft-runnings* got.
Laft droppings make but *Taplafh*, fuch as mine;
Your's is the boiling blood o'th' *lufty Vine*.
You fhine like *Planets* (thofe rich Lords of Light)
Out-braving us mean *Commons* of the *Night*.
I've fcribled out my *Helicon*---,afraid
The *Iffue* in my *Arm* has drain'd my *Head*.

Your praife is, *Penfion-like*, on me beftow d ;
Old, and decrepit now, that does no good.
By fuch advances tho, I keep in fight :
Thus can the *Moon* gild o re the *gloomy night.*
The *Name* I've wrongly got eife foon will fail ;
Tho *Hillocks* may feem *Mountains* in the *Vale.*

INCONSIDERATE LOVE. 1678.

Strephon's *Arguments to* Cœlia, *to forfake Youth, Wealth,
and Temperance, in his Rival, and to accept their
Extreams in him.* To **C. B. M.**

Love, that i' th' happy Age, a *Monarch* reign'd,
Is now by wealth in golden fetters chain'd.
His *Altars* once to *Merit* facred were,
'Till *Riches* turn'd the *World Idolater.*
Hearts now by pairs , are like to *Turtles,* fold ;
Love, Vowes, and *Sacrifice* all rul'd by *Gold.*
Now *Cælia,* now's the time to fhew your worth,
And from *Love's Temple* drive the *Bankers* forth.
For whilft you feek to marry pelf to pelf,
You buy a *Husband,* but you fell your felf.
    Fat foils bring *Weeds* ; the cleaneft *Corn* is found
In leaner *Fields,* if you well drefs the ground.
Tho more of coft, yet more content is had
To build a *Houfe,* than buy one ready made.
Philip of Spain did to no meannefs fall,
From *Cloifter poor* to raife th' *Efcureal.*
Scorn not poor *Strephon* : you may be o'recome :
The thred-bare *Gauls* o re-ran triumphant *Rome.*
Sure honour he muft gain in this hard Fight,
If he retreat not, whilft a *Crown's* in fight.

He

He need not fear *white Wiggs* nor *downy Chins,*
Who lose their leaves, before their fruit begins.
Yielding your self to such, you must decay,
And mony lend against your self to play.
There's no more dang'rous, no more frequent thing,
Than is a *Surfeit* of *raw* Love i' th' *Spring.*
When *Love* to his try'd *Stomach* must succeed,
And, like *digested meat,* new vigours breed.
Their ravenous Love, with active motions blown,
(Like *Fire*) consumes what e're it preys upon.
His flames yet burns not ; like *æthereal Fire,*
Whose nature is to last and to aspire.
Days may in *Winter* be both cool and fair;
And *Fires* in coldest Seasons brightest are.
Love may sometimes seem sleepy in his breast :
Souls thus tow'rds Night compose themselves to rest
But wake more fresh, and with new vigours blest.
Youths *burning-Feavers* make 'em restless lye,
Consume their loves in vi'lent heats, and dye.
His *Aguish-heats* are temper'd well with cold
Such *Loves,* like that *Disease,* will longest hold

See now, fair *Cælia,* neither *Wealth* nor *Youth*
Can true content secure, or vouch for truth.
In rich and beauteous *Meads* sweet *Flowers* grow ;
His craggy *Rocks* have precious *Stones* below
Unpractis'd Youth may lavish out Love's store,
Turn *Bankrupt,* and forsake you, being poor.
His *Age* will be so frugal not to waste
That treasure, but preserve it to the last.
No other *Rival* now sure dares advance.
Unless that thin-gut-chap- fall'n *Temperance.*

                                        Altho

Although your *Empire* great as *Cæsar's* were;
A meager *Cassius* you may juftly fear,
Abftemious Zealots ruin'd *England* more,
Than all its jolly *Heroes* did before.
  O *Cælia!* ne'r to fuch become a *Prey*;
  Make ufe of fleeting Joys whilft they will ftay;
  Since Life's confined to fo fhort a day.
A right *Good-Fellow* daily whets delight,
Returning briskly as to th' *Wedding Night.*
Life's fed with *Love*; as *Men* with *Oyfters* dine;
They cloy, if not digefted well with *Wine.*
Heightned with mirth, and Sack, he entertains
His *Spoufe,* with various forts of pleafing Scenes.
Wit's requifite in *Love,* as in a *Play*;
To recompence the labour of the Day.

These Virtues, *Cælia,* then in *Strephon* chufe;
And in all others their *Extreams* refufe.
Though he want *Wealth,* and *Temperance,* and *Youth,*
Yet he abounds in *Merit, Wit,* and *Truth.*
Or if to wed without thofe three y'are loth;
You have your felf enough of them for both.

The Perfect GENTLEMAN. 1678.

Upon the Death of the truly Honourable Gentleman,
John Howe, *Efq;* of Langar *in* Nottingham-
fhire, *my moft honoured Friend.*

EYes having done their parts, the *Tongue* muft fpeak:
  And tho loud *fighs* have made mine accents weak;
That breft muft yield a found, whofe *heart-ftrings* break.
             Their

Their griefs are moſt, who ſilently lament:
Such fires are hotteſt in their *Fornace* pent;
Yet fann'd by ſighs the *flame* now finds a Vent.

Thoſe ſad reverberating groans that riſe
Fro th' Caverns of my boſome, change their noiſe,
And, *Eccho*-like, diſſolve into a Voice.

No *ſhow'rs of tears* my *ſorrows ſtorms* can lay;
Nor ſighs (thoſe *guſts of grief*) blow tears away:
My life muſt be one *rainy-windy-Day.*

The Life of Man depends on breath in chief:
Chameleon-like, my ſorrows gain relief
Fro th' inward air of ſighs, that *breath of grief.*

Such ſigns of grief by *Nature* ſhould be ſent;
Since ſhe has loſt her choiceſt Ornament,
Her *Winds* in *ſighs, Rain* ſhould in tears be ſpent.

Both *Nature* and the *Graces* here combin'd
All beauties both of *Body* and of *Mind*;
Perfections, ſcatter'd through the World, here joyn'd.

So curious, ſo proportion'd every part,
That neither ſtrength, nor Beauty got the ſtart,
Hence *Durer* might have form'd more rules of Art.

Thoſe charming *Muſcles* that his ſmiles compos'd,
Were like the *Net*, which *Mars* and *Venus* clos'd.

Conſult but him---old ſtories did not feign;
Th' *Amazonian* Empire prov'd here plain ;
Beauty, and *Valour* did together reign.

Nor

Nor joyn'd they only in his outward frame ;
Their Virtues in his Soul too were the fame :
Like *Lightning* bright, but threatning was his flame.

So working in his *Breaft* his *Spirits* were ;
Had they been ramm'd in any breaft but there,
The weaker *Gun* had fhiver'd into Air.

His *Body* only his great *Soul* did fit :
And there alone his Soul could only fit :
Nature's right *Tallies* ! this, with that did hir.

His brighter *Virtues* we cannot unfold ;
Thofe that lefs dazling are we may behold ;
'Tis wife to fave the very drofs of Gold.

What we can comprehend, we here but write ;
We guefs at *Pyramids* above our fight,
And by their *Shadows* only take their height

So true a *Patriot* -- It was his care
His *Prince*'s and his *Countries* love to fhare ;
No *Favourit*, and yet no *Popular*.

So kind a *Husband*, his fair *Lady* knew
No carriage, but like that when he did wooe ;
All he did then pretend, he fince made true.

So good a *Parent*, it may raife debate,
Which of his gifts may claim the higher rate ;
Their Life, his great Example, or Eftate.

He was the braveft *Foe*, the trueft *Friend*,
That ever *Love*, or *anger* did pretend ;
Both which, with Juftice, did begin and end.

To

To all in want he favours did beſtow;
His *Charity*, like *Nilus*, did oreflow,
And made the neighb'ring barren Soyls to grow.

His *Converſation* pleaſant was, and good,
And like to *Iſraels* heav'nly *Manna* prov'd;
To all dilicious, yet ſubſtantial food.

Deſignd with Juſtice, by all-knowing Fate,
To all that Fortune gives both good and great:
Rich is the *Stone*, that without foyl is ſet.

How ſoon our hopes were bury'd in deſpair?
Thus *Fabricks* vaſt require no leſſer care,
Nor coſt to build, than keep 'em in repair.

Nature's great Gifts he nobly did requite;
The Splendors he receiv'd, he made more bright,
His *Diamonds* paid, as well as borrow'd light.

But we have loſt the comfort of his rayes;
This ſudden Cloud our Senſes did amaze:
Darkneſs ſeems moſt, after the brighteſt blaze.

Let us with ſadneſs his bleſt period view;
Sickneſs and *Pains* did ſo his Soul purſue;
As *Fate* would try what a *great heart* could do.

Too ſoon his lofty Soul did mount the Sky:
Spirits too faſt ſublim'd in vapours fly:
As richeſt men decay, that live too high.

Th' *eternal ſpark*, Heav'n kindled in his breſt,
By mortal damps could never be ſuppreſt;
But ſoar'd a *Phœnix* from its *flaming Neſt*.

So th' *sacred Lamp* (that was the *High-Priest's* care)
Long hid in darkness, when expos'd to th' Air,
Reviv'd its sleeping flame, and beam'd more fair.

His Soul (above the Sun's) scorn'd to set low ;
Its faculties ev'n then did bigger show :
As *Evening* shadows in dimensions grow.

His thoughts were greater, when *Death* came in sight
In those approaches to his latest Night.
H' inlarg'd his *Room*, to let in greater light.

With sharpest darts the *Tyrant* did assail ;
Against his *Heart of proof* none could prevail ;
It was so guarded with its *Native Mail.*

Bold *Scæva* thus, upon his *faithful Shield,*
Receiv'd a *Grove of Darts*, yet scorn'd to yield ;
Retiring great as *Cæsar* from the *Field.*

Prologue to Henry *the third of* France, *at the*
Royal Theatre. By Hart. 1678.

YOu're not t'expect to day the modish Sport,
    Affronting either *City*, or the *Court.*
Our *Poet's* mannerly, and cautious too,
And neither will abuse himself, or you.
Faith both are needless ; since they're done each day,
By you who judge, and he who writes a Play.
The sacred thirst for *Bays* and *Fame* is gone ;
And *Poetry* now turns *Extortion.*
Nay worse, *Stage-Poetry* seduces more
Than *Wine*, or *Women* ever did before

Gain

Gain'd by its charms, hither the Wits refort ;
The *Stage* robs both the *Pulpit* and the *Court.*
The other *Sex* too are ftark rhyming mad,
Ev'n from the *Dutchefs,* to the *Chamber-Maid.*
Nor do thefe Charms in the *North Country* fail,
But took our *Poet* both from *Hounds* and *Ale.*

His *Scenes* (fuch as they. are) in *France* are laid ; ⎱
Where you may fee the ancient *Englifh-Trade* ; ⎰
Either in beating *France* or giving aid.
Such Vertue reign'd then in our fmiles or frowns,
Thofe did defend, as thefe could conquer *Crowns.*
Thefe *Miracles* were in *Eliza*'s Reign ;
Whofe left-hand *France* and *Holland* did fuftain ;
And whofe right-hand both baffled *Rome* and *Spain.*
Whilft *England* only could the *World* fubdue,
Nay found a *new one* out, and reign'd there too ;
Judge then what now *Great Britanny* may do ;
Since now her *Helm* a greater *Pilot* guides ;
Who has th' advantage of his *Sex* befides.
Tho here our Poet rather would make known
His *Country*'s Reputation than his own ;
Yet he may chance by *Criticks* to be hift,
As he intrencht upon the *Cafuift.*
But he no *Controverfies* fets on foot ;
And thinks it better if none elfe would do't.
Nor tells you which *Religion* he is on ;
May be (like moft of you) he is of none.
If this prove true, he muft the *States-man* move ;
Then for the *Ladies* he has Scenes of Love.
And here *Gallants* are fighting *Scenes* for you ;
Nay, here is *Huffing* for you *Hectors* too.

What

What the pox, *Gentlemen*, would you have more?
Y'are cloy'd sure with the *Atheist* and the *Whore*.

Epilogue (*by a Woman*) *to the same Play, soon after
the Royal Theatre was fir'd.* 1678.

'TIS very hard, whilst *Fortune* was our Foe,
  You should diflert us for her being so.
We were your *Favourites*; and none before
Loft that Preferment by their being poor.
Small cause, that you should with that *Whore* conspire
To fend us *Famine*, 'cause she sent us *Fire*.
The *Scenes*, compos'd of *Oyl* and porous *Firr*,
Added to th' Ruine of the *Theatre*.
And 'twas a Judgment, in the Poet's Phrase,
That *Plays* and *Play-house* perish'd by a *Blaze*   }
Caus'd by those gaudy *Scenes* that spoil *good Plays*.

But why for this should we forsaken be?
It was our *House*, alas! was burnt, not *we*.
And yet from hence might some suspicion come,
Since it first kindled in our *lowest Room*.
The *Fire* did seize on all, both *Brick* and *Wood*;
But we more lucky were in *Flesh* and *Blood*.

If we be poor, what then? we're honest tho;
And that's the thing, we fear, that loses you.
If you, *Gallants* and *Ladies*, som times range   }
Fro'th' *other House*, it will not seem so strange;   }
You know the brisk delightfulness of *Change*.

Sure

Sure you, and they are cloy'd e're this : One *House*
Muft needs be dull and tirefom, as one *Spoufe*.
By long *Co-habiting*, and *Dowry* too,
They'l claim a *Title*, and a *Right* in you.
Nay worfe ; with *Age* they heighten ftill their fenfe,
Exacting more than due *Benevolence*.
In extream need fuch ufage to purfue,
Is damn'd *Extortion*, and ill *Manners* too.
For by this trick you may be half undone ;
If now, when all the *Miffes* are from *Town*,
Each *Suburb-finner* fhould exact a *Crown*.

The HERO. 1678.

To his Grace, the Duke of Monmouth, &c.

WHen *Wars* were rumour'd, or great dangers near,
Mars then was fought, his *Temples* crouded
From, You, great Sir, & from your *flaming blade*, (were.
Our *Eden* boafts her glory, and her aid.
Not *Eden* only with your beams you gild ;
But, like the *Sun*, fhine upon ev'ry *Field*.
'Tis duty then our *Lawrels* we fhould bring,
As *Off'rings* to the *Pow'r* that makes 'em fpring.
They 'mplore, great Sir, your Influence and your Aid ;
Lawrels themfelves ! of *Thunder* not afraid !

What *Gen'ral* e're began with more renown,
At once to guard the *Miter* and the *Crown* ?
Charls is our *Jove*, in's *Conduct* bleft we are ;
And *Monmouth* is his *Thunder-bolt* of War.

P   Wit

Witneſs the *French* at *Maſtricht*, who, with ſhame,
Kindled their Valours at his gen'rous Flame.
You were the ruling *Genius* of the *Field*;
Their empty *Veins* your Spirits only fill'd.
You taught 'em how to conquer, rais'd their Name.
'Twas you advanc'd their Trophies, lent 'em Fame.
Which on a brave deſign you did beſtow;
That is, to make them fit to be your *Foe*.

Rais'd by your Acts, at higher things they aim;
To follow *Monmouth* is the Road to *Fame*.
Europe, at their ſucceſsful *Arms* amaz'd,
Look'd pale, and all its trembling *Princes* gaz'd.
On *Britain*'s mighty *Monarch* fixt their Eyes,
Whoſe greater Puiſſance did more ſurprize.
For *Engliſh Conqueſts* ſwiftly'r might advance,
Since *England*, more than once, had conquer'd *France*
But then remembring *Charles*, as juſt, as great,
His help, as their laſt Refuge, they intreat.

Mons is beſieg'd, and ready to be ta'n;
Monmouth being abſent, other hopes were vain.
At your Approach the *Gallic* Flame expires:
Thus does the Sun put out the weaker Fires.
Your very Name did weary'd *Mons* releaſe,
Made the *French* fly, and truckle to a Peace.
Swift as the *Lightning*, and as piercing too!
Jove thus on's *Eagle* at the *Giants* flew.
The ancient *Romans* did ſome fear betray,
To pinnion *Victory*, and force her ſtay.
She, like their conqu'ring *Eagle*, courts your hand,
And will kill ſurer, by your Valour mann'd.

Wh

What e're fhe flies at muft your *Quarry* be;
Who can refift *Monmouth* and *Victory?*

The fi'ry *Mars* is pow'rful in his *Sphear*;
Yet lofes Virtue when concern'd elfewhere:
Our *Mars* a general influence can afford;
There is his *Sphear* where e're he draws his *Sword.*
In fuch Exploits *Cæfar* was never skill'd,
Firft to make *France* to conquer, then to yield.
Thus *Æolus* with his impetuous *Bands,*
Charging the *Lybian Defarts*, drives the *Sands*
Into a Mountain, which his *Trophy* ftands.
'Till changing fides, he rallies in the Air
His *Troops,* and then commands to found to War:
The lofty *Pageant* tumbles to the Ground,
And's *Trophy* now is in its Ruines found.

The MIRROR. 1679.

Prefented to the Honourable Mrs. Byron.

G'Ood *Fortune!* now at laft be fond;
And give me that bright *Diamond*
O'th' great *Mogul:* when it appears,
Sun-like, it routs his leffer *Stars.*
Here *Phœbus* fixing all his Rays,
Made it but one compacted Blaze.
It is fo weighty, that it's faid
To be by *Ounce,* not *Caracts* weigh'd.
As tho to leffen Pride, 'twas meant
For Burden, not for Ornament.

Had

Had I this *Gemm* (your Merits due)
It I would sacrifice to you.
Pure Incense! where no Smoke aspires,
Kindling it self with native fires.
But now, alas! I have not time
To post to so remote a Clime!
Nay, when at *Agra*, or *Lahore*,
May be, the *sullen Emperour*
Would keep his *Diamond*, I'le not try;
And yet speed better, tho more nigh.

Presents should hold proportion due
To th' Persons they are offer'd to.
And mine's a *Mirrour* darting rayes,
That *Diamonds*, and *Sun* out-blaze.
The *Chrystal* I this *Winter* chose
From drops of *Helicon* new froze.
The *Glass*, I, with some Art, design'd;
With *Truth* instead of *Silver* lin'd.
A *Lining*! that rich *Tissue* shames;
Brighter than are *Meridian* beams.
So heav'nly rich! to make em shine
It does the *Vests* of *Cherubs* line.

Being thus prepar'd, It snows to you
An Object worthy of your view:
Wit, Greatness, Virtue, Beauty, Worth,
At once in glorious *Crouds* break forth:
And from two shining *Casements* fly:
Like *Angels* shooting through the *Skie.*
Whose Rosie-blood, *Dame Nature* strains
Through *Lilly-cheeks*, amd *Violet-veins.*

Whose

Whofe *Scarlet*, *Lancafter* once wore,
His *Rofe* dipt in that precious ftore,
Turn'd *Red*, a *Damask-rofe* before.
Her whom I faintly here exprefs,
Your modefty denies to ghefs.
Untill my *Glafs*, being heav'nly true,
Reflects your felf, and fpeaks it you.

The H I E R O G L I P H I C. 1679.

To the Honourable Mrs, Byron, *having pleas'd to fend me curious and fignificant Draughts of her Ladi-fhips own hand, in way of* Hierogliphics.

COuld I, like you, my *Pencil* ufe ;
  Or had command of fuch a *Mufe* ;
All other *Artifts* I'd out-do,
By coming fomthing near to you.
But as poor *Dreamers* oft conceit,
Were they in fortune rich and great,
They'd live, and fpend at fuch a rate.
So had I your *Eftate* in *Wit*,
Like you, methinks, I'd manage it.
Pallas (that charming *Goddefs*) fhe
Should ferve inftead of *Mufe*, to me.
Inthron'd fhe fhould *Queen Regent* fit,
And better rule my frothy wit.
As pow'rful *Cynthia* both guides
Th' unruly *Sea*, and all her *Tides*.

Your drops of *Ink*, like thofe i'th' Spring
Both *Violets*, *Rofes*, *Lillies*, bring.

Your

Your *Fruit-trees* equal Wonders fhew;
Both bear at once and bloffom too;
The *Spring* and *Autumn*'s both in you.
Your planted *Vines*, i'th' infant Stems,
Seem to bud forth their blufhing *Gems*.
Apelle's felf would be mifta'en;
Both *Birds* and *He* could not refrain.
When you, with *Grafs*, cloath fancy'd *fields*,
They feed thofe *Flocks* your *Pencil* yields.
And what does greater Wonders fhow,
Your *Ink*'s the *Milk* that makes 'em grow.
When you draw *Birds* we wond'ring ftand,
And fwear they fly from out your hand.
Here *Tyanæus* Art is gain'd;
And we their Voices underftand.
When you a pleafant *River* limm,
Your *Ink*'s the *Stream* where *Fifhes* fwim.
Nature's Defects you here recruit,
And *Proverbs* crofs, they are not mute.
Your imitating *Pencil* can
Firft form, and then put Life in *Man*.
Each *Shadow*, *Rib-like*, can relieve
Your new-made *Adam* with an *Eve*.
Your Art, more ftrong than that of Fate,
Can livelefs things ev'n animate.
Your *Trees Dodona*'s influence fhare,
And are, like them, *Oracular*.
Your very *Shadows* fet out *Light*;
What is your *Day*, if fuch your *Night?*
Your *Pindust* is not vainly hurl'd;
Its very *Attomes* make a World.

You

You th' *Hieroglyphic*-Art revives
In *Egypt* dead, in you alive.
Thence *Learning* took it's happy flight:
So from the *East* first shot the *Light*.
What Admiration's then your due ?
How much is *Art* it self oblig'd to you ?   (too.
Since *Madam* you can make a *World* and it inlighten

MERIT Rewarded. 1679.

To the Right Honourable William *Lord* Byron, *upon
the Death of* Rich. *Lord* B. *his Father.*

ANcient has been the use to mourn in *Verse*;
   And *Poets*, more than *Heralds*, grac'd the *Herse*.
The sacred heat that did their Breasts inflame,
By *Muses* fann'd, kindled the breath of *Fame*.
Hence to diviner heights did Worth aspire,
And brighter shin'd than in the *Fun'ral Fire*.
To *Heroes* only did their *Verse* belong;
Immortal Acts found an *immortal Song*.
'Twas *Merit* then did only purchase *Praise*;
Nor could a *Crown* of *Gold* bribe one of *Bays*.
Your noble *Father* their choice Skill had try'd;
Had he in those days either liv'd or dy'd.
And though I am unfit to sing his *Name*,
This *Epitaph* I sacrifice to *Fame*.

The Epitaph.

ILlustrious *Byron* Justice found;
   Being four times crown'd.

1. From noble *Ancestors* did get
   A *Coronet.*
2. Then loyal *Valour* did bequeath
   A *Lawrel wreath.*
3. His Suff'rings *Martyrs* glory found
   With *Roses* crown'd.
4. Nothing can add to his great *Story,*
   But that of *Glory.*

My Lord,

I shall not vainly mourn his doom,
Since he dropt fully ripe into his *Tomb:*
Yet loaded more with *Glory* than with *Days,*
Hence with my *Cypress* then, and reach me *Bayes.*
My *Muse,* like to its Subject, should be bright,
And, like to *Roman Mourners,* clad in *White.*
When first his Death was told, her Tears she shed;
And, like moist *Lillies,* droopt her dewy head.
Pearls thus at *midnight* fall from *Luna's* eyes,
But are again dry'd up at *Sol's* uprise.

Hail then Restorer of our Joys! shine bright,
And with thy *Cynthia* joyn in *sheets* of Light.
Increase your noble *Stock:* Thus *Persians* say
The *Queen of Night* joyns with the *King of Day*
And, curtain'd in *Eclipses,* there they get
That *shining Brood* that in the *Skies* are set.

A R-

P O E M S. 217

ARREARS. 1679.

To the Honourable Mrs. Chaworth.

TO you I have such *Rents* to pay ;
   In Policy I should not stay ;
If from my self I knew to run away.

   Your *Cottage* tho is in repair ;
   The inward *Rooms* well furnisht are ;
The *Windows* glaz'd, and *Roof* new thatcht with *Hair.*

   Your *Tenant* clad in *Scarlet* Vest,
   Carouzing *Clarret* of the best
Within the *Lodging-Chamber* of my Breast.

   High fares he with no ill intent ;
   For if he starve,---You lose your *Rent* ;
Since none, but he, can farm the *Tenement.*

   My hopes of thriving are decay'd ;
   Wire-drawing Wit in Rhyme's my *Trade* ;
And I no store of *Bullion* have for aid.

   Small stocks in *Country* trades may do ;
   Ev'n *Pedlers* there deserve a view :
As little *Gold* beat thin will make a shew.

   A *smutty Fancy,* or *bald Jest,*
   Profaneness in *Hobb*'s Livery drest,
Serve for a *Session*'s charge, or *Churching-Feast.*

   This will not do in *London-Town* ;
   Not trusting without Money down
Hence are their very *Lawreats* Bankrupts grown.

Nor

Nor ftrange ; Times fo expenfive are :
The *Tripos* once requir'd lefs care
To manage well, than now a *Barbar*'s *Chair.*

To woo a *Lady* 'till fhe's fit,
Needs now more coft of Plot and Wit,
Than formerly to *wed,* and *Children* get.

Sack's influence once infpir'd the brain :
'Tis well if now it can maintain
Fit *Reparties* for th' *Drawers* witty Vein.

The *Coffe-houfes* now admit
More *Criticks,* than the very *Pit* ;
As prodigal of *Treafon,* as of *Wit.*

Befides all thefe expenfive ways ;
I lavifht out, and writ two *Playes* ;
Catching at *Hope,* I nothing got but *Bayes.*

Into the *Country* quite undone,
My *Mufe* and I, both *Bankrupts,* run :
Like wandring *Luther,* with his bare-foot *Nun.*

The R E N T due. *Jan.* 1. 1679.

To the fame.

L Aft years expence has made me frugal grown :
Your *Rent* I fav'd, altho fo long in *Town.*
Wit is not current now ; the humou'rs hot
I' th' *Town,* to talk of nothing but the *Plot.*
No *Age* a greater wonder hath reveal'd ;
The more difcover'd 'tis, 'tis more conceal'd.

Thu\

Thus some late *Poets* of their *Phœbus* write;
His *Highness* hidden is by too much light.
But lest my diff'rent fate (an obscure name)
Should prejudice the title of your *Claim* ;
I have survey'd th' *Estate*, and *Cottage* too,
In this short *Draught* I here present to you.

Three *Storyes* high, upon an *Arch* 'tis plac'd;
Two *Windows* in the *Front* with *Chrystal* glaz'd;
A double *Door* ; the Leaves of *Coral* made,
Which to the House, 'twixt *Rayls* of *Pearls* convey'd
A supple *Porter* in his *Lodge* does wait
To welcome every *Guest* that pass'd the *Gate*.
On either side the *Door*, two *Spots* of *Snow* ;
Discolour'd now, where *Roses* once did grow.
Two *Tunnels* to convey the thicken'd Wind,
Rais'd by the heat, not yet to flame refin'd.
Of *Bones*, the *Roof* did like a *Cruo* show ;
Thatcht o're with *Straw* that on the *Soyl* did grow.
Worn thin with time ; to keep out Wind and Rain,
The *Cupo* warmly coated is again.
The *bony frame* dawb'd with a *mud-wall* case,
Refin'd by th' *Fornace* of its native place.
The lower Rooms mean *Offices* contain,
And cleanly kept, through which the *Kennels* drayn,

I' th' second Story, Places choicely drest ;--
And first, the *Presence-Chamber*, where does rest,
In fitting state, the *Monarch* of the breast.
The *Dining-Room*, where *Ventiducts* are set
To bring refreshments for excessive heat.
And *Stoves* (which wisest *Nature* there did frame,
Like *Vestal-hearths*) to save the *dying flame*.

A sacred

A sacred *Fount* does in the *Center* rise,
Rich as the Spring that water'd *Paradise*.
Th' *Egyptian Queen* who quaft a *Kingdom* up,
Infusing *Pearls* into her wanton *Cup* ;
The *Draughts* compar'd, ours have by far the odds ;
This was the *Nectar* of the *Demy Gods*.
And looks as tho that blushing *Queen* of *Gemms*
(The *Ruby*) were dissolv'd into these Streams.
Hence *Princes* are in this rich *Colour* drest ;
Since *Life* it self shines in a *Scarlet-Vest*.

And now am I to the *third Story* come ;
The highest, and, alas, the weakest Room !
That once Experience would but cross the Jest,
And prove the highest *Chamber* furnisht best.
For *Knowledge* (*Nature's guide*) should quarter there,
And *Judgment*, her most trusty *Councellour*.
Invention, *Memory*, and *Wit*, should stay ;
And all their Treasures in this *Turrit* lay.
But for such *Guests* I have no fitting Room ;
Or if I had, I've no such *Guests* to come.
If you vouchsafe it, You must from your store
(Like *Princes*) send your *Furniture* before.

I've here design'd a *Draught* with little cost,
To stand a *Land-mark*, lest your *Claim* be lost.
And mighty *Purchasers*, for want of heed,
Oft' leave out petty *Parcels* in the *Deed*.
When *Alexander* did the *East* subdue,
(And he no *Conq'rour* was, compar'd to you)
Amidst his many *Trophies* of renown,
Summing the *Audit*, he had lost a *Crown*.

The

The PROROGATION. 1679.

To the Honoured Sir Scroop Howe, *Knight of
the Shire for* Nottingham-shire.

SOme good from *Prorogations* come ;
   Since, worthy Sir, they fend you home.
We *Country*-men did want you more,
Than did the *Courtiers* heretofore.
Your prefence will advance our fates,
As much as it has their *Eftates*.
Be kind to us, and no more give ;
They'l fuffer you at home to live.

Love is not only here more *true* ;
But it is alfo *fafer* too.
I' th' bargain they are much mifta'ne,
Who pay for pleafure and buy pain.
No *Popifh Plots* difturb our Nights ;
We fleep, or wake to fafe delights.
They furely find a dreadful ftate,
Who *burning* fear from *Love* or *Hate*.
No fawcy *Politicks* we read ;
Nor fhoot our bolts who fhall fucceed.

To *Law*, and *Gofpel* we refer it ;
Let them decide who muft inherit.
Who, without thefe, thinks of the *Crown* ;
We need not fight, nor pray him down.

We here hate nothing but the *French*,
Their *Wine*, their *Worfhip*, and their *Wench*.
                                    Welcom,

Welcome, dear Sir, to your true Friends;
Who love you only for your ends.
For your own worth you are defir'd;
By all, but by your felf admir'd.
Now, you are lov'd by more men here,
Than you, or I, lov'd *Women* there.

The WELCOME.

To the right Honourable the Lady Anne Howe.

THe archeft *Cheats* to *London* get,
    Yet *London* is the archeft *Cheat.*
Moſt there i' th' *gentle-craft* combine;
Both *Courtier, Lawyer,* and *Divine.*
Methinks, their arrogance is odd,
To rob both *King,* the *Law,* and *God.*
London ! repent for what is paſt;
Thou mak'ſt us fair amends at laſt.
You, Madam, and your health repay
All Treaſures, it e're took away.
For all the *millions* we have laſt,
Wee here get D*amages* and *Coſt.*
Your preſence will decay its ſtore;
And we ſhall now complain no more.
Then fit *Returns* muſt needs be ſought,
For all theſe bleſſings you have brought.
Our ſervices, our pray'rs, and we,
Long ſince were your propriety.
And tho all theſe belong to you;
Here we preſent 'em to your view,
Their claim of int'reſt to renew.

Then

Then, Madam, you can never fail
Of hearty *welcoms* from the *Vale* ;
The *noble houſe* from whence you came,
Vouchſafing *Honour*, and its *Name*.
Our *Joy* (that *health o'th' Soul*) we give
For th' *health* of *Body*, you receive.
But we have better things than theſe,
More worthy you, and fit to pleaſe.
To make this bold aſſertion good ;
Behold th' *Elixirs* of your blood.
Fair tranſcripts of your noble mind ;
Rich proofs *Sir Scroop* and *you* are kind.
Sure-vouchers of a future bliſs ;
Hopes of the next Age, Joyes of this.
May *Sons* and *Daughters* live t' inherit
Both *Father's* and the *Mother's* Spirit.
Love then may juſtly *Trophies* build ;
For they will ſurely win the *Field*,
When all, both *Men* and *Women* yield.

BEAUTIES MONARCHY. 1679.

To the Honourable Mr. Briget Noel,
vouchſafing a Favour.

VErſe, without truth, is a dark *Day* ;
    Where peeping glimpſes play,
Without the favour of one ſhining ray.

When Poets leave fictitious Dreams ;
    Apollo gilds their *Themes*,
Smiling upon 'em with auſpicious beams.

Accoutred

Accoutred thus, He courts your fight ;
And you reflect his light :
Like polifht *Chryftals* making it more bright.

The treafures of his blazing *Mine*
All objects elfe refine ;
Your *Eyes* alone gild o're his Silver fhine.

'Tis you out-influence the *Sun* ;
His *Charter* is out-done ;
You make me *Poet*, who before were none.

The *Statue* thus that *Memnon* made,
Was filent in the *fhade* :
Struck with the *Sun-beams vocal Mufick* play'd.

No greater Treafon can their be,
Than your own *modefty* ;
Refufing *Univerfal Monarchy.*

Apollo with his *Troops* tho ftands,
Like the *Prætorian Bands,*
Forcing the *Empire* on unwilling hands.

Inthron'd you fit on *glorious blaze:*
Difdaining *Lawrels, Bayes ,*
Glories incirc'ling you of your own *Rayes.*

Dazled to death by your fierce Beams,
We but refine our Fames :
Like *Martyrs* glorying in the purging Flames.

But if your pitty cool your Eye,
And will not let us dye ;
Like *Confeffors*, our Faith wee'l not deny.

W

With *Roses* then I shall be crown'd,
Tho *Bayes* cannot be found;
Living, or *Dying*, your *Rewards* abound.

I must be just, tho I am vain:
My *Conscience* bears no stain
Though zeal, for you, makes me a *Puritan*.

With all Devotion I confess
Beauty, than *Goodness* Less;
Yet yours so great, it would an *Angel* bless.

Your goodness tho must greater be;
Too large for *Quantity*;
Since, oh, it did vouchsafe to think of me!

Gifts then are duly entertain'd,
And in a right light stand;
When we regard the *Persons* whence th' are gaind.

In our *Inferiours*, *Bribes* they are;
To gain a better share:
As some for *Riches*, barter breath in *Pray'r*.

When from our *Equals* they are sent;
They are but favours lent
By *Tenants* to be stopt in the next *Rent*.

Superiours, in the meanest thing,
Not *gifts*, but *honours* bring:
As when a *Knighthood* is vouchsaf'd by th' *King*.

Yours, Madam, goes a higher rate,
And brings a richer fate;
Since you confer'd both *honour* and *Estate*.

Q   Great

Greater acknowledgments are due;
I owe my felf to you;
For you both grac'd, inrich'd, and bleft me too.
Bleft I muft be; for whilft I rate
The virtues of your ftate,
The *World* may fall in love, and imitate.
Infpir'd thus with a facred rage,
To be your *Poet* I ingage:
Then whilft I fing your praifes right,
The *World* will be converted by't,
And I the *Apoftle* of this Heath'nifh Age.

TRUE NOBILITY. 1679.

Upon the Death of the Right Honourable John
Earl of Rutland, *&c.*

THat *little God* within, the *fpark divine,* (fhine;
    Which does, i'th' *Body,* through the *Windows*
Whofe influence here dreffes us up a *Name*;
And, after *Death,* revives us in our fame:
Whofe fprightly *falt* preferves the *Body* whole
In all its *Parts,* 'twould elfe ftink out the *Soul*:
Which, whilft incarnate, is exactly dreft;
For *Scarlet* both keeps warm, and lines the *Veft.*
It is the *Sun* that makes thefe *Diamonds* bright;
Dark drops! till he has lin'd 'em through with light,
How vainly we employ our fenfual *Eyes,*
When we the beauties of the *Body* prize?
Ufelefs the *Lanthorn* is, and dark as Night,
When *Death's* cold blaft puffs out the trem'lous Light.
                                                    Whilft

Whilst tenanted, the *House* is in repair,
Built with *Mud-walls* of *Flesh*, and thatcht with *Hair*.
But when the *Tenant's* gone, 'tis ruin'd quite:
And who can stay *Death's* cold and darksome *Night*,
When *Fire's* extinguisht, and put out the *Light*?

Yet ruin'd *Temples* still command our care,
And *Stones*, that made the *Altar*, sacred are.
For common use they should not be profan'd,
But in some choice *Repository* stand;
Till by some pious resolution blest,
Once more they're fitted for the former *Guest*.

Great *Rutland's Relicks* may more rev'rence claim,
Than ever yet from *Superstition* came.
And 'tis but just--that we to *Altars* run,
Whence *Blessings* came, and *Miracles* were done.
What could from *Mannors* less expected be;
Sprung from Fourth *Edward's Royal Progenie?*
Great *York* to plant his *Roses* here thought good,
Painting their *Snow* with drops of *Mannor's blood*.
But least th'advantages of so much cost,
Should in those azure Labyrinths be lost;
A glorious *Mark* eighth *Henry* did bestow;
That future Ages might the honour know.
No greater favour could the fame advance;
Grac'd with the *Arms* of *England*, and of *France*.

But I disturb his *Dust* with these *bald Rhymes!*
Dust when interr'd, *Bells* cease their jangling Chimes.
Yet *Love, Respect*, and *Truth*, so fan my fire;
And from their flowing stores my breast inspire;

Q 2   That

That like the *Prophet*, they supply my *Muse*
(That needy *Widdow*) with a springing *Cruse*.
My *Standish* dreyn'd, the *Fountain* bubbles still;
The fruitful Subject thrives upon my *Quill.*
When other strengths, before their time, are spent:
As *Roses*, by long handling, lose their scent.

True heats of *Zeal* did in his *Actions* glow;
A warmth, that frozen *Age* does seldom know:
And yet his Spring was hot, for all his *Snow.*
Thus *Fires* o'th' *Altar*, that from *Heav'n* first came,
For many ages did preserve the flame.
His chearful looks did represent his mind;
Through *chryſtal* of his *Eyes* his *candour* shin'd.
Transparent were his thoughts, his virtues known:
Through *Tagus* streams, the golden *Sands* were shown.

His *Charity* fell like the *Morning Dew,*
As beneficial, and as constant too.
His pray'rs to Heav'n, from Heav'n did blessings gain:
As *Vapours*, sent from *Earth*, descend in rain.

This was the blessed *Circle* he did frame;
So went his Soul to *Heav'n*, from whence it came.
The tow'ring *Falkon* thus her self does skre w
In airy *Rings*, till almost lost to view;
Then perches on that *Hand* whence first she flew.
Whilst daily crouds his lib'ral *Alms* did gain,
How glorious he appear'd with such a *Train?*
Far more than those oftentuous *Pomps* now shown;
Begging the *Countrey*, to inrich the *Town.*

Whoſe

Whofe Goodnefs, like their Greatnefs, is more fhow ;
Like *Winds*, whofe Being's only while they blow.
Their *Names* are loft in the deep calm of *death* ;
And, *Vapour-like*, their fame fades with their breath.

Had I a *Wreath* of *Bayes*, I'd lay it down ;
And *Cyprefs* fhould my *Mufes* temples crown.
She, and her Sifters leave to boaft their pride
In their extraction, by the *Fathers*-fide ;
Lay by their *Vefts*, fpun of the *Morning* Rayes,
And trimm'd with *Mid-day-beams*, like *golden lace* ;
Courting their *Aunt*, (the *Queen of Night*) to gain
Mourning, of that fame ftuff did make her *Train*.
Accouter'd thus in fitting ftate fh'appears ;
Penfive as *Midnight*, all bedew'd with tears.

NEW LIBANUS. 1679.

To the Right Honourable Catharine *Countefs of* Rutland ; *Upon the Bleffings brought to that* (*wellnear-extinguifht Family*) *by Her felf and Honourable Iffue.*

Honour'd Madam,

IF I'm o're-bold, *Zeal* makes the errour lefs ;
For *Zeal* is but *Devotion* in excefs.
If it more forward preft than you requir'd,
'Tis my *Soul's* warmth by agitation fir'd,
Such *Zeal*, and true *Devotion*, are the fame ;
Or only differ, as do Heat, and Flame ;
That cherifhes it felf ; but *Zeal* incites
The World, to imitate its blazing lights.

Q 3   *Praifes*

Praises to sing, and *Powers* to admire,
Are the chief *Descants* of the *heav'nly Quire.*

'Tis fame enough, that I have led the way,
And tun'd the *Strings* for skilful hands to play.
They may advance th' inventions of my *Muse* :
As *Sciences* improve with time, and use.
In primitive *Professors,* all confess
Their *Zeal* devouter, tho their *Knowledge* less.
By no *Divinity* inspir'd, but you ;
I am your *Poet,* and your *Prophet* too.
Rare Subject ! where all *Poetry* may strain;
And never be asperst, that it does feign.
Where *Fancy* most exalted, seems to be
Plain *Demonstration,* and true *History.*
It easie is for *Prophets* to divine ;
When blessings clearly through your *Actions* shine.
Bright *Issue,* from such *Springs* as surely streams,
As *Sol* and *Luna* propagate their beams.

Belvoir's an *Orb* so great, Both there unite ;
And thence your *Infant-Stars* derive their Light.
As glorious, and as lasting, may they prove ;
Those hopeful *Products* of your mutual love.
Great-Rutland, with these *Prospects* clos'd his Eyes
And joyfull, like prophetick *Jacob,* dyes.

How should we celebrate your precious *Wombe* ;
That this Age blesses, and the next to come ?
Past Ages fitting recompences found ;
Bellies of fruitful *Princesses* were crown'd.

O! that

O ! that your *Royal Name-fake* could but fet
A *Crown* as fure, as you a *Coronet* !
Your pregnant *Soil*, rich as are *Indian Beds* ;
Where one *Rofe* blows, foon as another fheds.
Fruitful as flowing *Nilus*, that ne'r fwells,
But future bleffings to its *Country* tells.
Like *Gideon*'s *Fleece*, drencht with *Cœleftial dew* ;
Whilft tears are all the *Moifture* others knew.
By friendly *Fate*, your happy *Lord's* allow'd
To meet a *Juno* in a fruitful *Cloud*.
Fruitful as thofe i' th' Spring when bleffings pours,
Upon the Earth, and *Silver* melts in fhow'rs.

Nor are your poor, by thefe expences grown ;
No more, than *mid-day-beams* exhauft the *Sun*.
What iffues from your *Orb* adds to your fhine :
As fragrant *Bloffoms* crown the *Geffamine*.
You, by thofe dear reflections, are more bright :
So Stars (thofe *feeds o' th' Sun*) rob not his light.
Nay you are fairer, as more happy found :
Some *Seeds* there are improve the *Mother-Ground*.

You, than the *Foundrefs*, I fhould more have prais'd,
Since you uphold the *Fabrick* that fhe rais'd.
She, like *Pigmalion* did the *Image* give ;
But you the *Goddefs* are that makes it live.

B E L-

BELVOIR. 1679.

A Pindarick Poem ; being a faint draught of that most noble Edifice, with some Characters of the late Nob¹ Founder, Owners, and their Matches.

The DEDICATION.

To the Right Honourable Jo. *Earl of* Rutland. *&c.*

THE greatest Orator, and Statesman said M. T. Cic.
   (May be the greatest ever Nature made,
     Where grace design'd no aid)
That if a heave'nly *Guest* confin'd below,
   Might none o' th' shining wonders show ;
The fretting secret would corrode his mind,
   And, *Viper-like*, a passage find :
So some o'' th' *Wonders* that in *Belvoir* are,
   And *Belvoir'* self I must declare !
Tho my *Description* has not equal grace,
    Unworthy of the *Place* ;
    It may perform its trust,
   And serve to keep away *Time's* dust,
By closing it within this *Paper-case.*

Such draughts of *Poetry* let none reject ;
   Fancy is no vain *Architect* ;
    Building cannot make it poor ;
    Of shining *Quarrys* it has store.
Apollo makes, and then refines
Its unexhausted golden *Mines,*
Untill the *Treasury* runs o're.

Kings

Kings in mighty actions skill'd ;
And their Exchequers fill'd,
Then fit they are
Vaſt ſtately Pyles to rear !
Yet *Poets* can more laſting *Structures* build.

Armida's Caſtle will make good the boaſt,
Founded on poor *Taſſo's* coſt.
Our rambling *Braves* advance
The empty gayeties of *France :*
And yet the *Louvre* is not equal ſeen,
To th' *Pallace* of our *Fairy Queen*
Spain's vaſt Eſcurial is o re-whelm'd with ſhame,
When we *Sol's* glorious *Pallace* name,
Whoſe beauties yet are in their prime,
Tho built by *Ovid* in *Auguſtus* time *!*
A *Paper-building* ! but his *Ink* well temper'd all the *Lime*.

My Lord, I'm none of thoſe,
Who are ſo vain to think
That *Verſe*, with all its *Rhyming clink*
Hides folly more than *Proſe*.
Embroider'd Coats may make one brave ;
But neither hide a Fool or Knave,
For gawdy trappings did expoſe
Eſop's proud *Aſs* both to contempt and blows.
And yet we muſt confeſs
Dull proſe or *Ruſtick dreſs*
Conceals not ignorance nor makes it leſs.
Witneſs our worſer times ;
Paul's oratory ſuffer'd loſs,
By many an idle *Gloſs :*
As *David's Poetry* by *Hopkin* s Rhymes.

It

It matters not how we our thoughts reherſe,
Whether in *Proſe* or *Verſe.*
So we tranſcribe but right and fair,
What *Copies* of our Minds declare.
Honeſt Intents
Make Love and Truth their choiceſt Ornaments.

In theſe laſt days
The *Soul of Wit* decays!
Weaker its Efforts are ſeen ;
As is obſerved of the *Poets Bayes* ;
They are leſs fruitful and leſs green.
'Tis the World's Dotage ; and we grow
Leſs good, leſs healthy, and leſs witty too.
If Fate could any thing contrive
To croſs this *Rule* that is too true ;
This *Theme* would *Poetry* revive,
And make my *Fancy* brisk, and ſtrong, and new.
Such as great *Virgil, Lucan, Horace* writ ;
(Thoſe *Triumvirs* of Wit!)
That triumph'd over Ignorance ;
And by their Choice, not Chance,
An Empire rais'd ; to which all *Poets* bow,
From their days, ev'n till now.
And never *Rebel* did againſt their Laws advance.

Their ſtrengths of Thought were great ;
Aided by cœleſtial heat.
Their Brains were warm'd with praiſe,
Mecæna's Favours, and freſh Wreaths of Bayes.
Their *Heads* were *heated Stills* ;
And Spirits dropt from *Noſes* of their *Quills.*

But

But in thefe cooler days,
(And *Winter Evenings*, ah! are cold!)
The frofty humour of the Age benums
Our Brains, hence nothing flows but *Rhewms*;
Thin fickly *Products* of neglected Wit.
    For now rewards of Gold
      Are hard to get,
As that rare Stone that *Chymifts* fay produces it.
    Who can avoid Defpair and Rage,
        To fee
Cæfar, *Mecænas*, *Poetry*,
      Confined to one Age?
The two choice Bleffings from above,
      Are *Wit* and *Love*.
Love gains all Empire, makes the World fubmit;
Wit is *chief minifter* to govern it.
    Yet both thefe mighty things decay,
    And, if neglected, will not ftay:
    They bring all Bleffings from above.
This, this, methinks, fhould great and rich men move.
Without *Reward*, farewel both Wit and Love.

      But ftay!
    Before mine go away,
    I'll give one ftruggle more.
      If I expire,
My *Theme* can, like ftrong *Cordials*, reftore
      My wafting Wit,
      And cherifh it;
As Spirits numb'd recruit with fire.
Thus *Priefts* when they did *Oracles* record;
Thofe Pow'rs infpir'd, which they themfelves ador'd.
                To

To the Reader of the following Poem.

F*Avour* I shall not hawk to gain;
 The *Quarry* is already ta'n.
For all that can be done or said,
I largely am before-hand paid.
The *Fœtus* thus is paid i'th' *Womb*
For all its Services to come.
My Duty then thou should'st not blame,
Nor that this Smoak attests my Flame.
Enthusiasts cannot Pleasures own,
Untill they make their Visions known.
St. *Paul* himself was not content
Till he had publish'd where he went.
Heav'ns glory to the World appears,
Printed in golden Characters.
This *Subject* ought to have been writ
From such a shining *Alphabet*
The *Pen* made of a pointed Ray,
Shook from the *golden Wing* of *Day.*
Yet shining Works upon dark ground
Will more apparently be found:
Eclipses so make Gazers run
To look upon the darkned Sun;
And yet behind the Cloud he's bright,
Ne're lessen'd in his proper Light.
However I the *Story* tell,
Since pleas'd I have, I have done well.
An *Architect* should chiefly try }
To please the *Owner*'s Mind and Eye, }
But others only by the Bye. }

Yet, *Reader*, if thou favour grant,
I'll cherifh what I do not want.
It 'mongft my precious Stores I'll lay
For Refuge in a *ftormy* day.
A *Cloak* in Summer is not vain,
Since *Sun-fhine* days may end in Rain.

B E L V O I R..

A Pindaric Poem, *or a faint Draught of that ftately*
Fabrick; with fome fhort Characters of the Noble
Founders, Owners, with their Alliances. 1679.

I Muft not be
    A *Schifmatick* in *Poetry*;
Conform I will, and follow th' mode;
My *Pegafus* fhall amble in the beaten Road.
    Thou, noble Lord, fhalt be
    Mecænas and *Apollo* too to me.
    O that I could a *Virgil* be to thee!
    Vouchfafe that I may chufe
Thy fair and vertuous *Lady* to my *Mufe.*
And if at want of number fome repine;
Rapt with Poetick Fury, I divine
    Your Fervours fhall not reft,
    Till bleft
With *infant Mufes* to make up the *Nine.*
    Let *Belvoir* be
    Parnaffus then to me.
    At the foot of this bright *Mountain,*
    Springs a facred Fountain;   *The Cellar.*
                                   Whofe

Whose spacious Veins continually run
With precious liquor, passing *Helicon*;
   By which *Jove's Nectar* is out-done.
  Each *Butt's* a pregnant *Womb* of Wit,
Where Poetry lies in the *Embrio* yet:
Oh, for the *Butler* now to *midwife* it!

   Imperial Mount! we must allow
Another *Crown*, besides the *Castle*, to thy brow.
    Thy beauty, strength, and state,
   Are so incomparably great,
    That *Truth* it self must tell,
  'Tis pity, as it is impossible,
    That thou shouldst yield to Fate.
It cannot then a *Superstition* be,
   To say to thee,
  Illustrious Belvoir, hail!
 Thou Honour giv'st, and Title to a *Vale*
More pleasant, more rich, than that of *Thessaly*.

  Those *Stairs*, by which we to the *Castle* mount,
    We justly may account
   Conductive to more Glory,
  Than ever yet was read in Story;
Unless the *Patriarch's Ladder* step between;
And yet that only in a Dream was seen.
Look! how the *neighb'ring Hill* there swells with pride,
   Because it found the Grace,
    To have its place
  Next to the *Monarch-mountain's* side.
With sev'ral Shades of *Greens* 'tis quilted o're,
  And checker'd with delightful store

                Of

Of various Flowers,
The Off-springs of fresh *April* Showers.

Too much Irreverence would be seen,   *The Hill*
To observe the *Handmaid*, & neglect the *Queen*. *on which*
The *Atlas* of our hope! whose *Shoulders* bear *theCastle*
A *World* of Beauties and of Glories too ;   *stands.*
   Or it more likely may appear
      Olympus to our view.
Where *Jove* and *Juno* sit inthron'd ;
With lesser *Deities* incompast round.
   No *Mountain* ever nobler crown'd !
This *Castle* has more Blessings gain'd,
Than to be founded on a *Hill* of *Sand* ;
On barren *Rocks*, whose Precipices fright
   The Gazer from his wish'd delight.
Other mean *Hills* some despicable *Turrets* show,
   Like *Warts* upon a Brow.
Some like *Usurers* are seen,
Tho homely cloath'd, yet richly clad within.
   With *Sand* (plain *Russet*) clad,
      Or, what's as bad,
   A grass-green *Vest*, but so thred-bare,
That *Earth* (the *naked skin* o'th' *Mountain*) does appear.
Within 'tis true they may be rich and bright ;
   But, like the Sun at night,
Below our *Hemisphere*, their Beams are out of sight.

Our *Atlas* looks not shabbily and bare ;
   His *Arms*, *Thighs*, *Legs*, all cover'd are
  With a *rich mantle* of eternal Green,
  As in the other *Paradise* was seen.
               Our

Our *Mountain*'s vaſt and brave ;
With *Nature*'s *Architrave.*
Cornice, and *Freeze,*
Of ever green and fruitful *Trees* ;
Whoſe fruits intice
To hope, not loſe a *Paradiſe.*
When *Flora* is i' th' midſt of all her pride;
And all the *Trees* cloath'd on the *Mountain* ſide ;
How pleaſant tis to ſee them grow,
Each ſort in an alternate row ?
To ſee them imitate
The World's unequal fate ?
Some Heads, than others feet, more low ;
And yet they grow ;
And ſometimes are as uſeful and as fruitful too.
The *Bayes* and *Lawrels* on the *Mountain*'s brow,
Make a moſt noble ſhow.
With *Conquerours,* and *Heroe*'s *Wreaths* 'tis crow
As fits a *Mountain* above all renown'd.
Then on the top are ſeen
The lovely *Walks,* and ſtately *Bowling green* ;
Even on the tops of Trees,
Like to the *Gardens* of *Semiramis,*
In her great *Babylon,*
No greater wonders could be ſhown.
Our *Turrits* too we can diſplay ;
As bright, and glorious as an Eaſtern day.
Glories ! that never ſhadows know ;
And look, with ſcorn, on Clouds below !
Our *Mountain* outwardly is fine ;
Its Treaſures through the top does ſhi

It is an everlasting *East*,
Where a bright Sun has built her nest.
Rich Vale! thy fruitfulness exceeds all sense;
Blest with a double influence.
Thou must with plenty flow ;
Inricht by one bright Sun above, and this below.

Who ever views in starry Night,
The heav'nly *Champaign* fair and wide ;
With cloudy furrows plow'd on every side,
And sown with glitt'ring seeds of light.
If he survey the fruitful field,
And *shining Crop* around,
To tell how many *Bushels* it may yield ;
Numberless they will be found,
Hee'll find th' attempt more vain
Than to tell *Sands*, or drops o'th' *Ocean*.
For whilst, through searching *Tube* he pries,
To count the many *golden Eyes*,
That grace great *Juno's* azure Trayn ;
(For Poets of her *Bird* did stories feign,   *Skies*)
Those thousand Eyes were *Stars*, her *Ground* the
The more he looks, the more the number multiplies.
So *Belvoir's* wonders to display,
Is to count Attomes on a Sun-shine day ;
Less numerous than they.
The glorious Sun at Noon,
When in his flaming Throne he stands;
You may as soon
Scrape up his shining Treasures, that are hurld
About the World,
And hold 'em in your hand.
R   His

His vaſt *Revenues,* make not poor
The *Country,* but increaſe its ſtore:
So *Vapours* paid to th' Sun from every ground,
Purſt in a *Cloud* ; when th' Seaſon's fit
To open it ;
Then down the *Liquid Silver* pours
In fruitful ſhowers;
And pay es with intereſt the fields around,
Here you may ſee
The ancient *Engliſh Hoſpitality* ;
Where all their *Neighbours* ſeem o'th *Family.*
Here, like the *Patriarch's* feaſts,
Half of the World are *Gueſts.*
And ſo proportion'd is the care,
An equal plenty they prepare ;
The *Table's* loaded o're with choiceſt meats ;
And beautifi'd with delicates ;
Impoveriſh'd is the *Sea,* the *Earth,* the *Air.*

Look at that ſtately, and yet eaſie pride
O'th' ſpatious *Stair-caſe,* light as day ;
Yet eaſie to aſcend, as down to ſlide.
Bleſt fate! if erring mortals may
Find *Heavn's High-way,*
But half ſo *wide!*
None then can miſs
The road to bliſs;
Since both the left ſide, and the right,
Surely does guide, and kindly does invite
To *Paradiſe.*
Wherever now I caſt mine Eye,
Such lively *Pictures* I eſpy ;
Methinks, the *old Wifes* tale is not a L`ye.

This seems the *Gyant's Castle*, where
He seiz'd on all that did appear;
And being cruel, being strong,
His living *Guests* upon the *Walls* he hung.
 Observe those costly *Hangings* there;
How lively in their colours they appear:
The Spring is in the *Chambers* all the year!
 The *Gardens* above *Stairs* are seen;
The *Lillies*, *Roses*, *Violets* and *Grass*,
 Flourishing in their native place,
Are not so white, so red, so blew, so green.
Those *Images* i'th' *Tapestry* then note; Servants
 There's *Bignal* got upon his *Nag*, Names.
Sir Charles, *Tantarra*, *Bentley*, *Crag*,
 Has each a *Persian Coat*.
See the rich *Furniture* in all the *Rooms*!
Floors spread with *Carpits*, weav'd in *Turky Looms*!
 Beds soft, and costly, they may vye
With those whereon luxurious *Asian Princes* lye!
 And yet, most *noble Lord*, we find
 They do not captivate thy mind,
 So much as please thine Eye.
 In each place *Miracles* abound!
Rich *Parian Quarries* are in *Chimney Pieces* found.
 Belvoir! thou must the Worlds chief wonder be;
Since *Nature* is turn'd up-side down for thee.
The lofty *Firr* stoops down thy *Floors* to frame:
 And tho laborious *Miners* cry,
 That *Lead* does at the *Center* lye;
Thy lofty *Roof* is cover'd with the same.

Now

Now we are thither got, come let us try,
  If ever any Eye,
A nobler, or a richer *Prospect*, did espy.
  If hither the great Owner move,
    He need not envy *Jove* ;
Since all's his own, that does beneath him lye.
  Nor is the *Metaphor* too bold !
  For, Reader, if thou didst behold
  All his great things ; thou wouldst confess
  All *Metaphors* went less
Than these great truths, which stretch'd *Hyperboles* can
  Mind there the *Valleys* richly drest   (but express.
    With *Ceres* favours blest.
  That spatious *Corn-field* there behold ;
  Look how the *Wind* ruffles its Ears !
    Methinks it now appears
Rouling with *Waves*, like to a *Sea* of *Gold*.
    Now let us *Westward* try,
Where we those thick curl'd *Heads* of *Oaks* espy,
    Under whose shades are pleasant *Groves* ;
  Where if this rude degenerate Age,
  Were not debauch'd with lustful rage ?
Shepherds and *Nymphs* might exercise their loves.
  Amidst these *Groves*, is sometimes seen
  The *Castle's* and the *Woods* fair *Queen*.
  Who when (i th' Spring) she does there ride,
    (The *Spring's*, and *Nature's* pride.)
Diana, and her *Nymphs*, are quite out-vy'd.
    Hark ! hark ! what noise is that ?
  Some *Huntf-man* winding a *Recheat*.
Look how th' affrighted *Herd* (like to the rest
  O'th' World forsake a Friend distrest !

                                    Ther

There, there, the hunted *Buck* does go
So fwift, that *Swallows* fly more flow.
  The *Hounds* now follow !
  Liften to their Cry ;
  The *Huntf-men* ride, and hollow !
 If you truft either Ear or Eye ;
 Their ecchoing Mouths fright Thunder back,
 The fwifter *Steeds* out-ride the Rack
Of gliding Clouds, when *Tempefts* vex the *Sky.*
  Admire this gallant place !
Surrounded with a large, and noble *Chafe* !
The *Deer,* altho at liberty, here ftay ;
And, in mere gratitude ne'r go aftray.
  'Tis princely, and but feldom found
 Such *Herds* to breed ; And after feed
   Then hunt, and kill;
   And all this ftill.
  Ne'r out of his own ground.
  Thrufhes and *Black-Birds* in his *Bufhes* bred
  And only with his *Berries* fed :
Out of his vaft *Demefnes* they cannot fly ;
They hop upon his Ground, they hover in his Sky:
They were in his *Dominions* bred, and there muft dye.
  And what is more !
It has the bleffings of an inward ftore.
  Not as fome Beauties are ;
  Foolifh, and fair,
  And (what is fcandal now) as poor
  Remoteft treafures come
To make it fit for the great *Owners* home.
  Veffels in *China* made,
  That in th' improving Soil were laid ;

         By

By *Artists*, in the *Golden age* well known,
As the rich workmanſhip will own.
Skreens, and *Cabinets* here ſhine,
    That from *Japan* were brought ;
Such as *Europæan* Arts cannot deſign ;
Nor with its choiceſt treaſures can be bought.
Unleſs *Columbus*'s traffick hold :
Who *Lead*, and *Iron*, truckt for *Gold* ;
Or where a *Bead* of *Glaſs* was found
Fit value for a *Diamond.*
Such *Coſt* and *Furnitures* as theſe
May make the Stranger-Reader gheſs
    That I muſt either feign ;
Or 'tis a place for *Kings*, to entertain
    Their *courted Princeſſes.*

In its own ruines 'twas interr'd of late
    By violence, and hate
    Of *Rebels*, and conſpiring Fate.
No mortal force ſo ſtrong could prove,
One Stone from its foundation to remove,
    'Till *Bombards* came ;
Whoſe thunder and whoſe flame
Equall'd, if not excell'd th' *Artillery* of *Jove.*
Beſieg'd by thouſands it at laſt did yield
    As tho 'twas requiſit,
    No fewer hands ſhould ruine it,
    Than did it build.
In its own rubbiſh thus it lay :
    Until its noble *Dame*
    Deſign'd its frame ;
And rais'd a *Body* out of its own *Clay.*

The mighty *Infant* grew!
Until it was a wonder, and delight
To Paffengers, nay, to the very Builders view ;
And did command at once, and pleafe the fight.
The *Legs*, and *Thighs*, of maffy *Columns* made;
The *Sinews* of *tough Lime* all interlaid ;
Its *ribbs*, and *bones*
Of ftrong well-polifht *Stones* ;
And then its *lofty head*
(Near neighbour to the Skies,)
Was cover'd with a *Cap* of *Lead* ;
Of *Chryftal* were its *Eyes* !
In twenty years this great *Coloffus* to its height did rife.

Leave we to celebrate the *Cafe*.
Let us the *Diamond* adore ;
For fo was *Rutland's Countefs* ! nay, and more,
The very Soul of this great place.
Of humane things fee the event !
As't was the *Glory*, fo the *Monument*
Of the great *Foundrefs* ; who might be
Divefted of mortality,
Before, from her own *Horeb*, fhe to *Heav'n* went.
Tho Souls immortal are,
Yet as their Bodies do decay,
The faculties o'th' Soul are at a ftay,
And in th' infirmities o'th' Body fhare.
A large, and vigorous Body, asks a Soul
Of equal ftrength ;
Or elfe it will confume at length ;
Becaufe it can't th' unequal bulk controul.

So

So having rais'd this glorious *Frame*;
Thy noble *Mother* knew its bulk, and fame,
Requir'd a spirit suitable, to actuate the same.
    For now hers look'd more high;
Having done two such mighty things on Earth,
    To raise this *Pyle*, and give thee birth,
Her next great thing was t' obtain *Eternity*.
    Yet left thee in a state,
At once both to oblige the World, and **Fate**;
    If thou wilt her example imitate,
Thou the succeeding Age must bless
With a *young Lord*, as she with thee did this:
The noble Name of *Mannors* to perpetuate.
    How great a fate on thee depends;
And glorious Causes must have glorious ends.
    Thy fair *Confort* may,
With reason, all our expectations pay;
And we may hopeful of such blessings be;
    Nay more, may claim a certainty
From such a one as her, and such a one as thee.

    Little need is there to boast
Of Rarities, brought from the *Indian Coast*.
    Japan and *China*, though they be
The *Cabinets* o'th' *Afian Treafury*;
    We need not thither roam;
    We have more precious Stores at home.
    Boughton, thou canst prove this true
Boughton! the feat of noble *Mountague*!
    The spreading *Tree*
    Of whose illustrious *Pedegree*,

Boafts as from *Eden* it tranfplanted were;
 Whether you regard the *Root,*
  Or fhining *Fruit*
  That it did bear.
From *Sals'bury's* great *Montacute* it came!
 Of whom no further need be faid;
Under Fifth *Henry's Enfigns* he was bred;
 And at whofe dreadful name,
A *Marfhal'd Army* once of *French-men* fled.
 Nor could lefs expected be
 From *Third Edwards* Progeny.
Third *Edward!* that in *Creffy Vale,*
Firft made the *Golden Lillies pale,*
  To make a deeper *red.*
At laft, thofe ftreams of Honour ran
To *Boughton's Mountague,* as to the *Ocean.*
 Too large to be confined there,
It overflow'd the *Banks:* that noble blood
Swell'd like a Silver-ftreaming Flood;
  Until it did begin,
Two *Earldoms* more, to circle in;
Of *Sandwich,* and of *Manchefter.*
Manchefter fhall not imploy my Song:
The Truth I will not, nor the Mufes wrong,
 But both will purchafe fame,
 By *Sandwiche's* ennobled name.
Sandwich! our *Nation's Phœnix!* that expir'd
In flames; in his rich *Neft* was fir'd.
 None ever greater dy'd*!*
He the *Dutch-Navy,* with one *Ship,* defi'd.
He ftood the mark of the whole *War!*
Until our Navy were fecur'd from fear.

      Then

Then from his Ship did Smoke and flames arise!
What nobler fame
Can add to *Mountagu*'s great Name,
Than to fall *England*'s Boast, and *Sacrifice*?

What mighty hopes might needs ensue
From *Mannors* and from *Mountague*?
Mannors,! a noble Bud! so richly set
By all advantages of Fate;
It was thought worthy to inoculate
With a rich Branch of Great *Plantaginet*.
Swell'd was this hopeful Bud,
With the *red Roses* blood,
Strain'd through *Fourth Edward*'s Veins!
What remains,
To make it more renown'd?
With *France*, and *Englands Arms* tis crown'd!
Who better can such great *Atchievements* bear,
Than their great *Issue*, which do spring
By both sides, from a *King*
Related both to *York* and *Lancaster*?
Sev'n streams from this rich *Fountain* issu'd forth:
Sev'n Daughters hence deriv'd their birth:
Like the sev'n *Planets* that inrich the Earth.

Muse! thou that *noble Dame* hast crown'd with Bayes,
That did this princely *Fabrick* raise.
The Theme will rich requitals give,
If thou so long as she shall live.
Inroll'd in *Fame's Records*, then thou wilt last
'Till *Time* be past:
Till *Death*
Shall stop the *Worlds* last breath;

Till

Till all its wind be gone
And vaniſh in the tempeſt of a groan.
Thou now muſt ſing another *Name,*
That can perfume the breath of Fame.
That can command all praiſe,
And with eternal verdure bleſs thy Bayes.
Whoſe merits like her Eyes do ſhine
Whoſe Beauty's, like her Soul, Divine,
'Tis, *happy* Lord, thy *matchleſs Katharine!*
So much cœleſtial fire
Shines in her Eyes, as may inſpire
A narrower Soul than mine,
To be Prophetick and Divine.
Hence I declare, none ever was or is,
Nor ſhall be more inricht with bliſs,
Than ſhe, and Thou, and thine.
Were not my Theme another thing;
Oh! how would I her beauties ſing?
Ere long,
That glorious Subject ſhall imploy my Song.
Till when the Reader may,
By theſe faint glimpſes gheſs at day.
But ah! it is not meet,
Thy *Lady* ſhould lie in ſo courſe a *ſheet!*

Each *motion* has a grace;
Her *Preſence* charms at once, and does amaze.
Eyes heav'nly bright;
Where *Joy,* and *Love* are gilt with *Light.*
Complexion ſuch,
As Art could never touch:
Nor Nature yet has ſhown,
But here alone.

As

As Lillies white, dew-drencht as soon as born;
And clear as Blushes of the rising morn.
Fresh as when Peaches first their blooms disclose,
Sweet as the Bud, new brought to bed o'th'Rose.
And yet---Who would believe this curious *Cabinet*,
Than Chrystal clearer, and more rich than Gold,
Is scarcely fit for th' *Jewel*, that it does infold?

Wise *Providence* ordained *Fate*,
(*Fate* ! the *Vicegerent* here below ;)
For *Rutland* to provide a *Mate*,
Fitting in birth, in fruitfulness, in show ?
And such a one they did create,
Whose blood from honourable fountains flow.
From noble *Campdens*, and great *Lindsey's* Veins,
Her inward Scarlet shew,
Shall be preserv'd, whilst Time remains,
In a Succession great, and blest, and true.
Noel ! that with the *Norman Heroe* came ;
And aided his victorious claim ;
Thence gaining, and bestowing fame.
'Ere since,-- Great actions did convince
That Loyalty waits on the name.
True to the Crown, when up or down.
Exulting in this noble pride,
One, in the *Conquerours* service, got renown ;
And one i'th' Service of the *greater Martyr* dy'd.

Than *Lyndsey's Bertye* what can greater be ;
True Off-spring of great *Vere* and *Willoughby* ?
Valour and *Loyalty* attend each *Name* ;
Pretending equal claim
Fruitful in Generals is their fate,
Or in great *Officers* of State ;
And

And muſt this praiſe command ;
The *Berties* ready are to bring
One of their Houſe, to ſerve their King;
With a *Battoon*, or a *White-ſtaff* in hand.

Here let *Pindar* pardon me,
  If it can be a fault ;
Among ſuch warlike company,
  To make a *Soldier's* halt.

Upon the Right Honourable R. Earl *of* Lyndſey, *General under King* Charls I. *at* Edge-Hill *(great Grand-father to the preſent Counteſs of* Rutland) *and* Mountague *Lord* Willough-by, *his Son, beſtriding him, when fall'n in the Battel.*

GLory *!* thou brighteſt of alluring things;
That add'ſt a Luſtre to the *Crowns of Kings*;
A *ſhining Veſt,* by *Heroes* only worn,
More rich than that which gilds a *Summers* Morn.
In this *Attire* illuſtrious *Lindſey* ſtands
In *Keynton-fields,* before the *Royal Bands :*
Thus did the glorious *Michael* (arm'd with Light)
'Gainſt *Lucifer,* and his damn'd *Legions,* fight.
That Act (tho great) a leſſer Wonder brought;
A *Mortal,* like th' *immortal Warriour,* fought,
Not much leſs Honour here great *Lindſey* gain'd ;
Charles to obey, his *Army* to command.
  'Tis true, he dyd ; but conquer'd tho before:
That *Northern Mars (Guſtavus)* did no more.
Whoſe leſſer Fate th' advantage him deny'd
To have a noble *Witneſs* how he dy'd :
Two *Armies Lindſey* may for *Witneſs* call ;
And cruſht his Foes, like *Sampſon,* in his Fall.
  Nay, more than this *!* he had the brave Content,
To ſee his *Honours Heir,* and *Ornament,*
How *(Cocles* like) an Army he defi'd ;
And his fall'n *Father* bravely did beſtride ;

As

As, by that well-built *Arch*, he had some hope,
That Noble-ancient-falling *Pyle* to prop.
A Posture suited both those *Heroes* well;
Thus *Clytus* stood, thus *Alexander* fell!
Too true! he fell before the Fight was done;
His Conduct tho and brave Example won:
So Light is borrow'd from the setting Sun.
Those charming Beauties, *Victory* and *Fame*,
Courted his Favour with an equal flame.
With Grief distracted, when our *Hero* dy'd,
Each lay her down, and hugg'd his bleeding side.
Where ever since, fix'd by his powerful Charms,
They are *Supporters* to his noble *Arms.*

I now must claim the Reader's Vote,
After this *Prospect*, nothing's worthy note;
Unless it be
Great Lord, thy Piety;
Who not content, this stately *Pyle*
(The boast and glory of the Isle)
Should reach the Clouds, as tho it vies
Its shining Beauties with the Skies.
And yet *Heavens Gate*, the *House of God*,
(Wherein his *Oracles* make their abode)
Should have so mean a show,
And then the Castle be more low;
As Heaven did downward grow.
Nothing reserved to thy care,
But to adorn, and to enlarge
The *House of Prayer.*
Thrice happy thou! who hadst so blest a charge!
Altho the Glory and the worldly Fame
Are due to th' *Founders Name*;
The *Crown* and *Blessing* fell thy better share.
Stately ought the place to be
Where a *Princess* is inthron'd;
And who can justlier be a *Princess* own'd
Than that cœlestial Maid *Divinity?*

Hen

Here, *noble Lord*, is only known
A *Beauty* greater than thine own.
Here thine with Reverence attends ;
And every day rich Off'rings does bequeath ;
   Fragrant Incense of her breath ;
  Which form'd in Prayers, to Heav'n she sends:
  By paying Heav'n its Honours due,
  Fair Lady, Heav'n will honour you ;
    Increasing your renown ;
    And on your head will set
(More glorious far than *Rutland's Coronet*)
    An everlasting Crown.

  Why stay we longer ? let's remove.
  Since nothing now appears to th' Eye,
  More great, more noble, or more high,
Unless the *Palace* of *Æthereal Jove.*
Homeward then Muse, and *Northward* turn thine Eyes ;
To see that lofty Spyre of *Botsford* rise ;
    Under whose sacred Roof does rest
    More precious *Dust*, than e're was drest
    With costly odours of the *East.*
    Under a nobler *Pyramid*
    Egyptian Monarchs ne're were hid.
Those *wonders* of the *World*, did never hold
    Heaps of purer *Mold* ;
    Than what these *Monuments* infold.
    Not one attom of this *Clay*
    Is foil'd with any base Allay.
Whilst animated here the Bodies stood,
They kneaded were with pure, and noble blood ;
    Not vitiated with stains,
    That now pollute some Veins.
Here's golden *Sand* that once inricht the *Flood.*

    Lo *!* where the precious *Relicks* lye ;
  Ostentuous Ensigns of *Mortality !*

Reposited with cost and care;
  Like *China-ware,*
To be rais'd up more shining, and more fair.
 How great and stately are the *Tombs?*
For noble *Guests,* it's fit to have such noble *Rooms.*
 And tis but just, that so great state
  Attend their Fate;
 Who liv'd in *Palaces,* when dead
 In *Palaces* are buried.
  Nor is this all !
If you will look on that *Historic* Wall,
 You'l into admiration fall :
That we no Chronicles of those times need,
 If we but these *Inscriptions* read.
 Each *Epitaph*'s a spatious page,
And tells the great remarks of its own age.
The noble Acts of all these *worthies* here,
With *Englands* acts, so complicated were;
As each was the *Intelligence* to *Brittain's Sphear.*
Most fit *Records,* such glorious *Names* to hold;
Whose *Leaves* are *Marble,* and whose *Ink* is *Gold* !

There is no fitter place to bid *Farewel,*
  Than in this blessed *Cell;*
 Where free from vexing cares,
Thy noble Ancestors, thou, and thine *Heirs,*
  Can only dwell.
 With my great Theme inspir'd,
 And with *Poetick fury* fir'd,
 Another *Prophecy* I frame :
 None of thine here shall come,
 As none yet hither came;
 'Till they made up the total sum
 Of *Honour,* and of *Fame.*   (Name.
And only with the *World* shall end thine *Honour,* and thy

FINIS.